GRE® 5-Hour
Quick Prep

for
dummies®
A Wiley Brand

GRE® 5-Hour Quick Prep

by Ron Woldoff, MBA

A Wiley Brand

GRE® 5-Hour Quick Prep For Dummies®

Published by: **John Wiley & Sons, Inc.**, 111 River Street, Hoboken, NJ 07030-5774, www.wiley.com

Copyright © 2024 by John Wiley & Sons, Inc., Hoboken, New Jersey

Published simultaneously in Canada

For general information on our other products and services, please contact our Customer Care Department within the U.S. at 877-762-2974, outside the U.S. at 317-572-3993, or fax 317-572-4002. For technical support, please visit https://hub.wiley.com/community/support/dummies.

Wiley publishes in a variety of print and electronic formats and by print-on-demand. Some material included with standard print versions of this book may not be included in e-books or in print-on-demand. If this book refers to media such as a CD or DVD that is not included in the version you purchased, you may download this material at http://booksupport.wiley.com. For more information about Wiley products, visit www.wiley.com.

Library of Congress Control Number: 2023951028

ISBN 978-1-394-23340-3 (pbk); ISBN 978-1-394-23342-7 (ebk); ISBN 978-1-394-23341-0 (ebk)

SKY10064102_010524

Contents at a Glance

Table of Contents

Start Here

The GRE challenges your ability to conjure up everything you've forgotten since high school — things you haven't thought about in years. Really, all you need is a refresher, some strategies, and practice. This book has all that and more: It goes beyond rehashing what you've learned (and forgotten) by providing exam-specific strategies and tips for answering questions quickly and getting through the exam. There are examples, practice questions, and practice exams to help you hone your skills, identify areas you need to work on, and build your confidence for test day.

About This Book

GRE 5-Hour Quick Prep For Dummies helps you prepare for the exam in 5 hours by breaking the basic things you need to know into five blocks that add up to five hours:

>> **Block 1 (20 minutes)** provides an overview of the GRE basics — what you need to know before you sign up, what to bring to the testing center, what to expect on the test, some general strategies, and how to interpret your score.

>> **Block 2 (1 hour)** helps you prepare for the essay and Verbal section. Learn what the GRE essay evaluators are looking for and how to provide the writing sample they want. You also explore the different types of questions you'll see in the Verbal section and find tips for how to answer them.

>> **Block 3 (2 hours)** reviews math — a lot of math. The good news is that most of this math isn't difficult if you understand the concepts and strategies explained in this block.

>> **Block 4 (1 hour, 30 minutes)** is a shortened practice exam that helps you simulate testing-like conditions while still keeping your preparation time within 5 hours. The answers and explanations help you check your work and dig a little deeper into the concepts you need to understand to succeed on the test.

>> **Block 5 (10 minutes)** is quick list of things to do the night before. This is the block where I tell you to relax because you completed the other blocks and are ready for exam day.

Basically, this book prepares you for the exam by taking your skills from the basic level to the GRE level and fixing any gaps. What else is there?

There's vocab.

To help you with vocab, as you work through this book, you'll notice that some words have a style all their own. Each GRE vocabulary word in this text appears in *this font*, followed directly by its *connotation* (meaning). Besides that, when you encounter a GRE vocab word in a question, look up its meaning and write it down. This is an effective complement to studying from a list or flash cards.

Foolish Assumptions

Since starting my test-prep company, I've had students who would be my boss in the business world, and many have gone on to have amazingly successful careers. You, too, are in this group of future success stories. How do I know? Because you're on your way to an advanced degree, which will open lots of doors, and you're oh-so-close to getting started. You just need to get past this one hurdle called the GRE.

That said, I assume you forgot almost everything the GRE asks you to do. This book covers the basic math and verbal concepts and offers challenging GRE-level questions. You also discover how to approach these questions, avoid common mistakes, and practice the intuitive tricks that help you knock it out of the park.

Even if you're a little rusty here and there and could use a few tips, I also assume you'll pick it up and do just fine. Succeeding on the GRE is like any other skill: If you know what to do, have some coaching, and practice, you'll likely achieve the score you need.

Icons Used in This Book

Look for these icons to spot highlights throughout this book:

This indicates a key strategy or point to remember. There are lots of these, which is good, because they're essential to your success on the exam.

This indicates overall knowledge about the exam that's useful for planning your approach, such as managing your time or knowing what to expect.

This marks a GRE trap or common student mistake so you can spot it and dodge it on test day.

This indicates a practice question for you to try.

Where to Go from Here

You can approach this book in two ways:

>> **Work through it from beginning to end.** This approach is best for most test-takers. Although prepping to take the GRE isn't a linear process, I present topics from easy to challenging, so they build on each other as you progress through each block.

>> **Skip around.** If you're especially nervous about a specific part of the GRE, jump right to that block, and you can start preparing for the test in the way that will help you become most confident on test day.

I've been helping GRE students beat the test for years, so I know not only students' common questions and mistakes, but also how to make the math and verbal questions easier to answer. This book distills my tricks and secrets, which I'm pleased to share with you. Your success, after all, is why we're both here.

Block 1

GRE Overview in 20 minutes

The GRE isn't an IQ test, nor is it a measure of your worth as a human being or a predictor of your ultimate success in life. The GRE is designed to assess your ability to excel in grad school by sizing you up in three areas.

>> **Work ethic:** How hard you're willing and able to work to achieve an elusive academic goal — in this case, performing well on the GRE — reflects your work ethic. Graduate schools consider this to be a measure of how hard you'll work in their programs.

>> **Study skills:** How well you can master some basic study skills and be able to process and retain new information.

>> **Test-taking ability:** How well you can perform on a test, under pressure, which is a separate ability from being able to answer the questions. Exams are *ubiquitous* (appearing everywhere) to grad school, so you need to prove that you can take one without folding under pressure.

This book can guide you in the first area, but it's mostly up to you. As a study guide, however, this book shows you how to achieve in the second and third areas, enabling you to study more effectively and efficiently and improve your overall test-taking skills. By knowing the material and taking the practice tests, you establish a foundation for doing well on the GRE. And usually, if you know what to do and how to do it, you might find yourself working a little bit harder. In this way, this book helps you further in that first area.

In this chapter, I discuss what you need to know about signing up for the GRE, the GRE's structure, some test-taking strategies, and the GRE's scoring system. With this guidance, you're better equipped to avoid surprises that may throw you off your game.

Signing Up for the GRE

When you sign up for the GRE, you have to decide whether to take the test in a testing center or at home. If you need accommodations or financial assistance, the GRE has a process you need to understand and follow. After walking you through some tips for both of these options, this section explains how to sign up for the test.

Choosing when and where to take the test

You can take the GRE at a testing center or at home. Because the computerized GRE is administered to individual test-takers, testing centers tend to have few seats, and those seats fill up quickly during peak admission deadline months (April and November). If you're planning to take the GRE in a testing center (as opposed to at home) around these months to get your test scores in on time, schedule your test early and secure your ideal time slot. You can always reschedule, but the last thing you need is an inconvenient time or location. Before at-home testing was available, I had a student wait until the last minute to schedule his exam, and he had to drive from Phoenix to Tucson (about 120 miles) to take his GRE and get his scores in on time. He called me during his drive, and we reviewed math formulas, but this wasn't an ideal way to ramp up for the test.

At the time of this writing, the at-home GRE test is an option. You will have to submit proof that you're not set up to cheat. ETS provides detailed requirements when you sign up, but anti-cheat measures include taking a video of your room and using software that ensures no other app is open on your computer. This may be invasive, but ETS has to make sure you're not stealing an advantage with your at-home setup. You also have to use a small whiteboard or laminated sheet for your scratch work, along with a dry-erase marker for your scratch notes, instead of the traditional pencil and paper that you get at the testing center.

Some students prefer the testing center so there are no home-based distractions (such as family, dog, or phone notifications). On the other hand, at-home testing ensures you can grab a time that works best for you, rather than selecting from the remaining open time slots at the testing center. Give it some thought and go with what works best for you.

Applying for accommodations

If you need an accommodation or financial support, the folks at ETS are usually accommodating as long as you give them a heads-up. Following is a brief list of special circumstances and how to obtain assistance for each.

REMEMBER

>> **Learning disabilities:** These disabilities refer to attention deficit hyperactivity disorder (ADHD), dyslexia, and other related or similar conditions. To find out whether you qualify for accommodations or a disabilities waiver of any sort, contact ETS Disability Services, Educational Testing Service, P.O. Box 6054, Princeton, NJ 08541-6054; phone 866-387-8602 (toll free) or 609-771-7780 (Monday to Friday, 8:30 a.m. to 5:00 p.m. Eastern Time), fax 609-771-7165, www.ets.org/gre, or stassd@ets.org.

Qualifying for accommodations is an involved process that takes time, and gathering the required documentation may require significant effort on your part. If you have a qualifying disability, act sooner rather than later to find out what's required and when you need to submit your request and documentation.

>> **Physical disabilities:** ETS tries to accommodate everyone. Folks who need special arrangements can get Braille or large-print exams, have test-readers or recorders, work with interpreters, and so on. You can get the scoop about what ETS considers to be disabilities and how the disabilities can change the way you take the GRE in the *Supplement for Test Takers with*

Disabilities. This publication contains information, registration procedures, and other useful forms for individuals with physical disabilities. To get this publication, send a request to ETS Disability Services, P.O. Box 6054, Princeton, NJ 08541-6054. Or better yet, head to www.ets.org/gre and click the Test Takers with Disabilities or Health-Related Needs link for all the info you need to know, along with contact information if you have questions or concerns.

>> **Financial difficulties:** Until you ace the GRE, get into a top-notch graduate school, and come out ready to make your first million, you may have a rough time paying for the exam. However, fee waivers are available. Note that the waiver applies only to the actual GRE fee, not to miscellaneous fees such as the test-disclosure service, hand-grading service, and so on. Your college counselor can help you obtain and fill out the appropriate request forms. (If you're not currently in college, a counselor or financial aid specialist at a nearby college or university may still be able to help you. Just call for an appointment.)

Registering for the test

REMEMBER

If you plan to take the GRE at a testing center, sign up early so you can choose the day, time, and place that work best for you. The time-slot availability varies per testing center, so if one testing center doesn't have a time slot that works for you, you may be able to try another nearby testing center, or you can schedule the test for home.

To sign up for the GRE, see the current *GRE Information and Registration Bulletin* (available through most college admissions offices), register online at www.ets.org, or register via phone by calling 800-473-2255. You can also check the GRE testing center locations and available time slots at www.ets.org.

TIP

To get into the right mindset, take at least one practice test at the same time of day that you plan to take the real thing. (Check out the practice test in Block 4.) If you're used to eating or relaxing at a certain time each day, make sure these tendencies don't sneak up on you during the exam. A recurring theme of this book is to make the exam and testing experience as familiar as possible, so that you're used to it and it's almost no big deal. (See Block 5 for more on gearing up for exam day.)

Knowing What to Expect on the GRE

On the morning of the exam, there's no such thing as a pleasant surprise. This section helps you avoid these surprises so you know exactly what to expect on exam day. This way, you can focus on the GRE in a more relaxed and confident frame of mind. Confidence comes from being prepared, and the last thing you want is to show up rushed and stressed *before* starting the exam.

Following the exam-room rules

If you take the GRE at a testing center, you must bring certain things and leave other things behind in order to be allowed into the testing room. Here's what you need to get together the night before the exam.

>> **Photo ID:** Your identification needs three key elements.

- A recognizable photo
- The name you used to register for the test
- Your signature

Usually, a driver's license, passport, employee ID, or military ID does the trick. A student ID alone isn't enough (although it works as a second form of ID in case something's unclear on your first one). Note that a Social Security card or a credit card isn't acceptable identification.

» **Water and a snack:** You may want a refreshment before you start the exam, so bring a bottle of water and a light snack, such as an energy bar or a granola bar. If you're like me, you'll have a to-go cup of coffee. Avoid snacks high in sugar, simple carbohydrates, or fats.

» **Map or directions:** Know in advance where you're going. Map your directions, and it doesn't hurt to check the satellite view so you can see where to park. You could drive to the testing center a few days before to check out the drive time, parking fees, and so on. If you're taking public transportation, find out where and when you need to board the bus or train, how long the ride is, how much it costs, and where you get off.

One student had to take the test at a center in the middle of a downtown area. She had checked out the area on a Saturday, when the streets were empty and parking was clear. But her exam was Monday morning, when the streets were jammed and the parking was taken. Naturally, she wasn't expecting this, and it was an extra stressor that morning.

TIP

Another option is Uber or Lyft. When Google Mapping the route to plan your trip, be sure to set the ride time to *the morning of the exam* so the trip time reflects the traffic. It doesn't hurt to plan on being there 30 minutes early, so if your driver or friend is late or doesn't know the roads, you have a time cushion.

» **Comfortable clothes:** Dress in layers. Testing centers can be warm, or more typically, cold. Shivering for hours won't help your performance. Dress in layers so you can be comfortable regardless of how the testing center runs the A/C.

» **Authorization voucher from Educational Testing Service (ETS):** If you pay with a method other than a credit/debit card or have a disability or require certain testing accommodations, ETS provides an *authorization voucher*. Not everyone gets this voucher, but if you do, be sure to bring it with you on the day of the test.

Just as important as knowing what to bring to the testing center is knowing what not to bring. Leave these things at home or in your car:

» **Books and notes:** Forget about last-minute studying. You aren't allowed to take books or notes into the testing center. Besides, if you don't know the material by that time, cramming won't help.

» **Calculator:** You aren't allowed to use your own calculator, but an on-screen calculator is available during the math sections of the exam. One nice thing about the on-screen calculator is that it features a button that transfers the number from the calculator field to the answer space. Your handheld calculator won't do that.

» **Friends for support:** Meet them after the exam. However, having a friend drop you off and pick you up isn't a bad idea, especially if parking is likely to be a problem, such as at a downtown testing center.

» **Phones, tablets, or other electronics:** Any electronic device, including your phone or iPad, is strictly prohibited. You can bring these to the testing center, but they stay in a locker while you're taking the GRE.

» **Scratch paper (at the testing center):** You aren't allowed to bring in your own scratch paper; the testing center provides it for you. If you run low during the test, request more from the proctor. Although you have plenty of room to do calculations and scribbling, your scratch paper stays at the testing center when you're done.

>> **Scratch paper (at home):** Note that if you take the GRE at home, you're not allowed to use paper of any kind, or pens or pencils for that matter. Plan ahead and pick up an ETS-approved small whiteboard or laminated sheet to write on, along with an erasable marker and eraser. At the end of the exam, you'll hold the erased whiteboard or sheet up to the camera to show the proctor that all your notes have been erased.

If the thought of bending these rules to give yourself an extra edge on the test even enters your mind, banish that thought. Cheating on the GRE simply doesn't work, so don't even consider it. They're on to you. When you get to the testing center, and before you begin your test, the proctors separate you from anything that you can possibly use to cheat, including your phone, wristwatch, water bottle, jacket, and hat. On top of that, you're monitored by a camera while taking the test. Any semblance of privacy goes right out the window. How would you cheat anyway? You can't copy all those vocabulary words or write all the math formulas on anything accessible during the test. Besides, the GRE tests your critical-reasoning and problem-solving skills more than your memorization skills.

REMEMBER

If you test at home, the GRE has controls in place to keep you honest. ETS monitors everything from the software on your computer to the electronics in your room. Be careful, and make sure you follow the rules — even a misunderstanding could cost you your score. Refer to the full set of rules on the At Home Testing page at www.ets.org.

WARNING

Someone caught cheating can be banned from taking the test for up to ten years! In the world of college education, that's nearly a lifetime.

Surveying each section of the GRE

Standardized tests tend to bring on the chills. Telling someone you have to take the SAT, ACT, or GRE usually gets the same response as saying that you need to have your wisdom teeth pulled. However, with this book, the GRE isn't such a chilling experience, and breaking it down to its component parts makes it more manageable and less threatening.

Table 1-1 provides a quick overview of what's on the GRE. The essay is always first, but the multiple-choice sections may be in any order.

TABLE 1-1 **GRE Breakdown by Section**

Section	Number of Questions	Time Allotted
Analyze an Issue	1 essay	30 minutes
Math (2 sections)	27 questions	47 minutes
Verbal (2 sections)	27 questions	41 minutes
Total Time		**1 hour, 58 minutes**

REMEMBER

At nearly two hours plus time spent checking in, the GRE challenges your stamina as much as your ability to answer the questions. No matter how solid your math and verbal skills are, you have to maintain your focus for the whole stretch, which isn't easy on a challenging task such as this. If you need to build your test-taking stamina, complete the blocks in this book so they add up to two-hour sessions. If you have extra time after completing this *GRE 5-Hour Quick Prep For Dummies*, you can take one or two free, timed practice tests online at www.ets.org/gre/test-takers/general-test/prepare/powerprep.html.

The GRE allows you to skip questions and return to them later, within that section. When you reach the end of a section, the GRE displays a review screen that indicates any unanswered questions. If you have time remaining in the section, return to these questions and answer them as well as you can. This feature is nice because you can knock out the easy questions first before spending time on the hard ones. (See "Understanding General Test-Taking Strategies" later in this chapter for more details about managing your time and flagging questions for review.)

Math question types

So what types of questions can you expect on the GRE? On the Math sections, you'll see the following types of questions mixed throughout the test:

>> **Multiple-choice with exactly one correct answer:** You know a multiple choice question has only one answer because the instructions tell you to pick one answer and the answer choices are marked with an oval.

>> **Multiple-choice with one or more correct answers:** Other GRE questions go overboard with multiple-choice. You can select more than one answer, and you have to get them exactly right: A missed answer or an extra answer costs you the point, and there's no partial credit. When you have one of these questions, the instructions always tell you to pick *all* correct answers, and the answer choices are marked with a square.

Note that with the squares, there could be one right answer, or two or more, or even all of them. The correct answer will never be *none* of the choices, though: You always have to select *something*.

>> **Fill-in-the-blank with the correct answer:** Some GRE math questions aren't multiple-choice. Instead, you type the answer into a box. This process isn't much different from a multiple-choice question: You still have to answer it, but instead of selecting your answer from a list, you type it into a box. Here are a few things you need to know about fill-in-the-blank questions on the Math section:

- **Rounding:** The question may ask for the answer to be rounded, such as to the nearest *whole number*, as in 13 instead of 12.8, or the nearest *tenth*, as in 3.7 instead of 3.72. Watch for these instructions, and remember that 0.5 rounds *up*. 4.135 rounds to 4.14, not 4.13.

- **Fractions:** If the answer is in the form of a fraction, such as 2 over 3, the answer entry will have two boxes, one over the other. Naturally, with this example, you'd place 2 in the top box and 3 in the bottom one. Note that an equivalent fraction is considered to be correct: If you type 4 over 6, or 20 over 30, you'll get the answer right.

- **Possible answers:** Sometimes a question has more than one correct answer, commonly in algebra topics. If x can equal 2 *or* 3, simply enter *one* of the answers in the box, and don't worry about the other answer. Your answer will be correct. Note that the question typically reads something like this: "What is one possible value of x?"

- **Answers with percentage or dollar signs:** If the answer is $42 or 37 percent, the question typically instructs you to disregard the percentage or dollar sign when entering your answer. The dollar sign is a no-brainer; simply enter 42 for $42. But the percentage can trip you up. Remember that 37 percent as a decimal is 0.37, *not* 37. Pay attention to whether the question asks for the answer *as a percentage* so that you're sure to answer correctly.

- **Calculator's Transfer Display button:** The GRE on-screen calculator has a button marked Transfer Display. You click this button, and the computer transfers the number from the calculator's display right into the typed answer box. Amazing! But be careful. To expand on the previous point about not mixing decimals with percentages, if the answer needs to be a percentage, and you correctly calculate 0.15, clicking Transfer Display places 0.15 in the answer box, whereas the computer is expecting the equivalent answer of 15 percent, which you should enter as 15.

>> **Data Interpretation (based on graphs):** A single set of graphs. These questions aren't harder, but they take more time to figure out because of the graphs.

>> **Quantitative Comparisons:** These questions tend to be based more on the math concept than the math calculation. You review two quantities side by side and select the one that's greater. For these questions, you always see the same four answers choices:

- Quantity A is greater.

- Quantity B is greater.

- The two quantities are equal.

- The relationship cannot be determined from the information given.

Verbal question types

The GRE Verbal sections have a totally different set of question types. Here's what you'll see on these sections of the test:

>> **Text Completion:** A Text Completion question consists of a sentence or paragraph with one, two, or three missing words or phrases, along with a short list of word or phrase choices to complete the text. If the text has one word missing, the list has five choices, while if the text has two or three words missing, each blank has a list of three choices.

Each choice gives the text a different meaning. Your job is to choose the word or words that best support the meaning of the sentence. If the text is missing more than one word, you don't get partial credit for choosing only one correct word.

Text Completion questions tend to have slightly easier vocabulary but are more challenging to interpret.

REMEMBER

>> **Sentence Equivalence:** A Sentence Equivalence question consists of a single sentence with exactly one word missing and a list of six choices to complete it. Your job is to select the two words that fit the sentence *and* mean the same thing, and, as with the Text Completion questions, you don't get partial credit for choosing only one correct word.

Sentence Completion questions tend to be easier to interpret but have more challenging vocabulary. The correct answers are *almost always* synonyms. If you find a word that works well but doesn't have a match, then you've likely found a *trap answer*.

TIP

>> **Argument Analysis:** You've probably heard the expression, "You can't believe everything you hear." That's what Argument Analysis is all about: challenging arguments and plans that you read in books, magazines, newspapers, and on the web; examining assertions that you see on the nightly news; and questioning claims that you hear from politicians, not to mention sales pitches. Graduate schools expect you not only to read with understanding but also to apply critical thinking to sort out what's supported by the facts and what isn't.

An Argument Analysis question consists of a short passage and a single question, though it may also appear as one of the Reading Comprehension questions. An argument is easy to spot because it presents a plan or a conclusion based on a set of facts. Your job is to determine what new fact strengthens, weakens, or completes the argument.

>> **Reading Comprehension:** Each Reading Comprehension question concerns a single passage that is sort of like a graduate-level journal article on a science, social sciences, or humanities topic that you've probably never considered before and never will again. The computer screen is split, with the passage on the left and a question on the right. You get the questions one at a

time while the passage stays in place. The GRE presents each question in one of the following three formats:

- **Multiple-choice:** Choose one answer only.
- **Multiple-choice:** Choose one or more answers.
- **Sentence-selection:** Choose a sentence from the passage.

Note that the question types are mixed throughout the sections, so you may encounter them in any order. Sometimes the software groups similar questions at the beginning or the end. For example, if you're halfway through a Verbal section and haven't seen a Text Completion question, you will.

Understanding General Test-Taking Strategies

As I mention at the beginning of this chapter, the GRE is not an IQ test, a measure of your worth as a human being, or a predictor of your ultimate success in life — but it is, at least in part, a measure of how well you take tests. If you understand and practice the test-taking strategies outlined in this section, you'll build the test-taking skills you need to score well on the GRE.

Planning question time

Don't obsess over giving each question a specific number of seconds, but do know when to give up and come back to a question later. A good rule of thumb is about a minute per question. As long as you haven't exited the section, you can return to any question in that section. Simply call up the Review Screen by clicking Review, click the question you want to return to, and then click Go to Question. You can mark a question for review so it's flagged on the Review Screen, or you can write the question number down on your scratch paper. Just keep in mind that while you're on the Review Screen, the clock still ticks.

Eliminating wrong answers

If a question has you stumped for the right answer, you may still be able to identify answers that are obviously wrong. After you eliminate any wrong answers, you have a better chance of choosing or guessing the correct answer.

For pointers about choosing the right answer on the Verbal section, see Block 2. For help answering Math questions correctly, see Block 3.

Throwing a mental dart

A wrong answer and no answer count exactly the same towards your score, so you may as well pick an answer. If you're not sure how to answer a question, *don't get stuck on it.* Instead, throw a mental dart and take a guess:

- >> Rule out as many obviously incorrect choices as possible, and guess from the remaining choices.
- >> Write down the question number or mark it for review, so you can return to it before time runs out on that section.

>> Finish the section, even if it means throwing more mental darts (in other words, taking more guesses) near the end. Because a wrong answer counts the same as no answer, you may as well guess and take the chance of getting it right.

Note that this is not really your main strategy. You should be prepared and able to answer most, if not all, of the questions correctly. But you may see a question or two that you're not sure how to answer. If that happens, just guess.

Flagging and reviewing questions

To gain experience with the computerized GRE, take it for a test drive using the free practice exams from ETS. At the time of this writing, the practice exam package is web-based and features two actual GRE computer-based practice exams for you to become accustomed to the format of the real thing. Access the POWERPREP Online at www.ets.org/gre/test-takers/general-test/prepare/powerprep.html.

TIP

The ETS practice exams look and feel exactly like the real thing, except that they don't hold your life in the balance. Most buttons are self-explanatory, but the following Mark and Review buttons deserve special attention.

>> **Mark:** Mark enables you to flag the question for review, and when you click it, a small check-mark appears on the button. Click it again to remove the checkmark. That's all it does.

When you mark a question for review, if you haven't answered the question, be sure to guess an answer! That way, if you run out of time, you at least have a shot at guessing it correctly. (See the section "Throwing a mental dart" for more on this.)

>> **Review:** Review takes you to the Review Screen, which shows a list of questions in the section, along with which have been answered and which are flagged for review using the Mark button. Select any question from the list, click the Go To button (which is only on that screen), and you're back at that question. You can then review the question and change your answer if desired.

A common trap is marking every question that you have the slightest doubt on, intending to go back to it later. Problem is, when you've reached the end of the section, you have 16 questions marked and only four minutes to work on them! Be sure to prioritize what you truly want to go back to.

Take the computerized practice test from ETS not only to get a feel for the content and format of the questions but also to become accustomed to selecting answers and using the buttons to navigate.

AVOIDING THE EXIT OR QUIT OPTIONS

When you take the GRE, understand what these two buttons do and know you likely want to avoid them:

• **Exit Section:** This button ends the section and saves your essay or answers so you can proceed to the next section. After you click this button, you can't go back to change answers or return to unanswered questions in the section. Unless you're really sure you've proofread your essay as much as you can or correctly answered and reviewed all the questions, don't click Exit Section.

• **Quit Test:** This button ends the exam and cancels your scores. Don't use this one. If you feel like you're not doing well on the test, keep going anyway to get the practice. You've already paid to take the test, so it's only to your benefit. "Seeing or canceling your scores" later in this chapter explains a better way to cancel your scores.

Understanding Your GRE Scores

With the GRE, you receive three separate scores: Verbal, Math, and Analytical Writing. You drive home knowing your unofficial Verbal and Math scores (as explained in the following section), but you get your Analytical Writing score about two weeks later.

On the GRE, you can score a maximum of 340 points on the multiple-choice and 6 points on the essay. Here's the scoring range for each of the three sections.

>> **Verbal:** The Verbal score ranges from 130 to 170 in 1-point increments. You get 130 points if you answer just one question, but that won't help you much: You need to score as well as or better than most of the other test-takers to improve your chances of being admitted to your target school. Block 2 gives you the lowdown on the Verbal sections.

>> **Math:** The Math score also ranges from 130 to 170 in 1-point increments. Block 3 has more on the Math sections.

>> **Analytical Writing:** The Analytical Writing score ranges from 0 to 6, in half-point increments, with 6 being the highest. For more details about the essay, see Block 2.

REMEMBER

If a multiple-choice question requires two or more answers, you have to get all the answers correct: There is no partial credit. However, you don't *lose* points for a wrong answer, so if you're not sure, take a guess and return to the question later.

Understanding how Math and Verbal scores are calculated

Within each section, each question counts exactly the same toward your score: The more questions you get right, the higher your score for that section. An easy question is worth the same as a hard question. Because you can move back and forth among the questions within a section, one strategy is to skip around and answer all the easy questions first, then go back and work the hard questions. If you like this idea, *try it out on a practice test* before exam day.

The *second* Math or Verbal section becomes easier or harder based on your performance. For example, if you do extremely well on the first Math section, the GRE makes the second Math section harder. Even if you don't get as many right answers in the second Math section, your score will be good, and it'll definitely be higher than the score of someone who bombs the first Math section but gets them all right in the second one. GRE scoring accommodates for the difficulty level of the questions in the second section.

WARNING

The strategy of bombing the first Math and Verbal sections in order to answer more questions correctly on the respective second sections is *not* a good one, and you'll end up with a low score. The exam doesn't score you based solely on the number of correct answers: It scores you based on how hard it thinks you worked and how well you studied to understand complicated material. So if you do *great* on the first Math section, the exam thinks you've worked hard and studied well to prepare for the test and *ups* the difficulty level for the second Math section. If you don't answer all those questions correctly, that's okay: The questions are harder, and the exam has evaluated your skills. Conversely, if you *bomb* the first Math section, the exam thinks either you're not good at math or you haven't worked hard and studied well for that section, so it *drops* the level for the second Math section. If you answer most of those questions correctly, it doesn't help your score much because those questions are easier.

Checking your score

If you score close to 340, you did great! If you score closer to 260, not so much. But wait — your score is right in between! Did you pass? Did you fail? What does it mean? Well, you can't really tell much about your score out of context. What does 320 mean? It all goes by a percentile ranking. To download the complete percentile table, visit www.ets.org, click GRE Tests, and search for "percentile ranking." As of this writing, here are some highlights:

>> A raw score of 165 is typically a 96th percentile ranking in the Verbal and an 84th percentile ranking in the Math.

>> A raw score of 160 is typically an 85th percentile ranking in the Verbal and a 70th percentile ranking in the Math.

Basically, with a range of only 40 points per section among 500,000 GRE-takers per year, give or take, each point counts for a lot. How well you do is based on how well the other test-takers did. You need to ask your target school's admissions office what score you need to get in to that school — or, even better, what score you need for a scholarship! Once you're in your program (or you've landed your scholarship), your GRE score doesn't matter. Plus, I've had students who were already accepted to their schools but were retaking the exam for the scholarship.

Also, your exam score is only one part of the total application package. If you have a good GPA, a strong résumé, and relevant work experience, you may not need as high of a GRE score. On the other hand, a stellar GRE score can compensate for other weak areas.

Seeing or canceling your scores

Immediately after finishing the GRE, you have the option of either seeing or canceling your Verbal and Math scores. Unfortunately, you don't get to see your scores first. If you *think* you had a bad day, you can cancel, and your scores are neither reported to the schools nor shown to you. However, the schools are notified that you canceled your test. If you choose to see your score, you see it — minus the essay score — right away, but you can't cancel it after that.

REMEMBER

How much do the schools care about canceled scores? Probably not much, especially if a strong GRE score (from when you retake the test 21 days later) follows the notice of cancellation. If you really want to know the impact of a canceled score, check with the admissions office of your target school. Each school weighs canceled scores differently. See the section "Using old scores" for more about what to do after canceling your GRE score.

Taking advantage of the ScoreSelect option

At the end of the test, you have the option of choosing which test scores to send to your target schools, assuming that you've taken the GRE more than once. You can send the most recent scores, scores from the past (within five years), or all your test scores. However, you can't pick and choose sections from different testing dates. For example, if today you did better in Verbal but last time you did better in Math, you can't select only those sections — you have to send the entire test. Select whether to send the scores of today's test, any previous test, or all your tests.

Your GRE score is good for five years after your testing date, so if you use ScoreSelect, you're limited to exams within the past five years.

Using old scores

What if you took the GRE a long time ago when you thought you were going to grad school and then opted to take a job or start a family instead? Well, if it was within the past five years, you're in luck (assuming you scored well). GRE scores are reportable for up to five years. That means that if you're pleased with your old score, you can send it right along to the school of your choice and say *adios* to this book right here and now. However, if you took the test more than five years ago, you have to take it again, so hold on to this book.

Block 2

Tackling the Essay and Verbal Tests

In this block, you find out what the GRE evaluators want to see on your essay and how they want you to think through the different types of questions you'll see in the Verbal questions. I give you tips for successfully completing both parts of the exam, and you find some sample questions at the end of this block that help you try what you've learned and check your understanding.

Writing an Essay Well and Fast

The GRE starts with an essay exam in which you're asked to analyze an issue. You're given 30 minutes to write your essay before you encounter any other test question. As you prepare for the essay-writing portion, remember these overall goals:

>> Write a well-organized, insightful essay that showcases your perspective and critical thinking.

>> Pace yourself and complete the essay within 30 minutes.

>> Write well and clearly, with few errors.

>> Conserve your energy for the rest of the test.

Thirty minutes for an essay is plenty of time *if* you know what to do and *if* you've practiced. The more you practice, the more comfortable you'll become with organizing your thoughts and expressing them in words within the time limit and under the pressure of the exam.

In this section, find out the writing and time-management techniques you need to give the essay evaluators what they want. I also guide you through the process of writing each essay, paragraph by paragraph. You can try an essay prompt and check your work against a sample essay in the upcoming section "Exploring a sample essay."

REMEMBER

On the GRE, you type your essay in a text box not unlike Windows Notepad or Mac TextEdit with formatting turned off. It features cut, copy, paste, and undo, but that's it — no spell check, grammar check, or automated anything, so the burden of proofreading is on you.

Writing the Issue essay

In the Analyze an Issue task, the GRE gives you an issue statement and asks you to introduce and then support your position on that issue. The format is like this:

TIME: 30 minutes

Today's cheap, mass-produced goods lack the precision and quality of yesterday's hand-built, carefully crafted products.

DIRECTIONS: Write an essay in response to the preceding statement in which you discuss the extent to which you agree or disagree with the statement. Explain your reasoning in a clear, well-organized essay that supports your position. Consider both sides of the issue when developing your response.

Where do you begin? What do they want? Only 29 minutes left! Getting started is the hardest part, and staying focused is the most important. With a game plan and a structure in place, you're equipped to do both. There are many strategies for writing a good essay, but this approach is effective and you can quickly master it:

1. **Read and understand the prompt.**

2. **Identify examples you already know about the issue.**

3. **Take a position that's in line with your examples.**

4. **Write a four- to five-paragraph essay using the following outline as your guide:**

   - **First paragraph:** Introduction stating your position

   - **Second paragraph:** Your best supporting detail

   - **Third and possibly fourth paragraphs:** One or two more supporting details

   - **Final paragraph:** Conclusion reiterating your position statement from your introduction

Step 1: Read and understand the prompt

The Issue Analysis essay prompt consists of an issue statement followed by instructions that tell you exactly what to do. The issue statements vary, and so do the accompanying instructions. Here are a few examples that illustrate how the instructions in Issue Analysis prompts may differ:

>> Write a response expressing your agreement or disagreement with this statement and the reasoning you followed to arrive at your position. Be sure to consider ways in which the statement may or may not be true and how these considerations influence your position.

>> Write a response expressing your agreement or disagreement with this statement and addressing the most compelling reasons and/or examples that may challenge your position.

>> The prompt may consist of a statement and a response, like a brief two-part conversation. In that case, the instructions may look like this:

Which do you find more compelling: Group A's assertion or Group B's response to it? Write a response in which you take a position and explain the reasoning you followed to arrive at your position.

TIP

At the time of this writing, ETS has made its entire pool of Issue Analysis topics available at www.ets.org/content/dam/ets-org/pdfs/gre/issue-pool.pdf. You don't have to type this whole address in your browser. Just include the word "pool" in your online search: "GRE issue essay *pool*." The list contains all the issue statements along with examples of the instructions that accompany those statements so you can develop a better feel for how the prompts may be worded and what they're likely to instruct you to do.

You can use this list for extra practice, but don't get bogged down by trying to practice on every topic — there are a *lot* of topics. Just read through some of them so you know what to expect. (We play a game in class called "topic roulette," where we scroll through the list, randomly pick a topic, and then as a group discuss the essay. I've had students tell me later that the prompt they got on the exam was one we reviewed in class!)

Step 2: Identify examples you already know about the issue

Your first inclination may be to state your position on the issue and then try to come up with data to support it. This may work, but it may also backfire. I've seen students take a stand and then struggle to support it. You don't have time for soul-searching or rewriting your intro a bunch of times. On the actual GRE, this approach would earn you an essay score of 2. Instead, find your supporting details and then base your position on those details. This way, no matter what, you can support the point you're making, and the evaluators check off the first thing on their list.

Before taking a position, use your scratch paper to write down five supporting details related to the issue statement. Along with each supporting detail, write down which side of the issue you think it supports. For the earlier prompt on handmade versus mass-produced goods, such a list may look something like this:

>> Your mass-produced Casio wristwatch versus your uncle's handmade Patek Philippe — favors cheap manufacturing

>> An off-the-rack suit versus a tailored suit — favors handmade quality

>> Your HP computer versus your friend's custom-built PC from catalog-ordered parts — can go either way

>> The $60 Raspberry Pi pocket-sized computer — can go either way

>> Your Toyota 4Runner versus your great grandpa's Ford Model T — favors mass production, but this example can easily be refuted by discussing the technology

TIP

Don't worry if your examples aren't perfect — you're racing the clock, so just throw down some ideas. You need only two or three examples, so writing down five gives you room to discard a couple.

Your examples can be taken from personal or professional experiences, your reading, or other general background knowledge you possess. What have you seen, done, or heard that formed your opinion on this issue? You may find that your examples support the opposite of your initial response; you want to discover that before writing the introduction.

Step 3: Take a position that's in line with your examples

From your examples, formulate your position. I know, you may feel like you're working backwards, but you want to take the position that you know you can support. This essay isn't a personal statement — it's a test of your ability to compose a clear, coherent train of thought. In this case, your best examples favor cheap manufacturing over handmade quality. So run with that, even if you personally disagree. If necessary, adjust your personal position for the essay. Your goal isn't self-expression; it's to score a perfect 6.

You're not making a commitment here. You're simply writing an essay to be graded. No one is going to bring this essay up in ten years when you're running for office. In fact, no one sees your essay ever again, and believe me, students and I have tried. If your supporting examples don't fit your inherent position, this half hour isn't the time for self-discovery about why or why not. Your task is *one thing*: Write a Level 6 essay. It's okay to declare something that you don't feel. Just look at your examples and write from a position that these examples can support.

The examples you wrote in Step 2 give you a good sense of where your essay will go. Now that your examples are down on paper and you've gathered your thoughts, you're ready to write your introduction.

Step 4: Write your Issue essay

You've laid the groundwork for writing your essay. You've read the statement and the instructions, identified supporting details, and shaped your position. The time has come to write your essay. The easiest approach to composing a great essay is to structure it around a very basic four- or five-paragraph outline, as explained in the following sections.

FIRST PARAGRAPH: THE INTRODUCTION

Use the first paragraph of your essay (the introduction) to demonstrate your understanding of the issue and clearly state your position. Structure the paragraph as follows:

>> **First sentence:** Introduce the issue and state your position as a response to the prompt.

   Take a *clear stand* in your essay — it's one of the things they grade you on. Arguing both sides of an issue, discussing strengths and weaknesses, or writing "It depends on the situation" is fine, but you must — *must* — make your position clear and be *consistent* throughout your essay.

>> **Second sentence:** Acknowledge the presence of both sides of the issue and that you, in fact, anticipate and address objections to your point of view while alluding to your brilliant logic and reasoning.

>> **Next few sentences:** Prepare the reader for your supporting details.

>> **Final sentence:** Write your thesis statement, which *uses words from the prompt*.

Repeat your thesis, with varied wording, at the end of each paragraph. You get points for being organized, and this is a good way for you to check that your example is on topic.

Refer to this bulleted list as you read the following example to see how I use this structure.

> The broad assertion that all mass-produced goods are inferior to handcrafted products is clearly overreaching, and I disagree with the statement. Certainly, in some instances handcrafted products are superior, but in other instances mass production yields more precise, higher-quality products. A few real-world examples, including a wristwatch, a suit, and a personal computer, demonstrate why many, but not all, of today's cheaper, mass-produced goods have better quality and precision than yesterday's hand-built, carefully crafted products.

A common pitfall is launching into the examples while you're still in your introduction. Then, when you get to the paragraph where you describe the example, you have nothing left to say. Such an approach demonstrates a lack of organizational skills and will tank your score. Instead, allude to your examples by mentioning what you *will* talk about in just a few words. Look at the sample introduction to see what I mean.

As you write your introductory paragraph, adhere to the following guidelines:

» **State your position clearly and succinctly.** The evaluators favor a concise writing style. If you can clearly state your point with fewer words, do it. That said, be thorough when making your point.

» **Convey confidence.** You're stating a position and supporting it with relevant examples. You know you're right, so act like it.

» **Stay on topic.** Digressing and expanding your scope to support your position is tempting, but keep your discussion within the scope of the issue topic. For example, mass production may lower the cost to reach a broader market, but the issue is about quality, not cost or sales. Anything outside the scope of the issue will result in a lower score.

» **Reference key terms.** The essay prompt describes mass production, quality, and precision, so use those terms whenever possible, especially in your thesis as the concluding sentence of each paragraph. Doing so signals that you're responding directly to the prompt.

SECOND PARAGRAPH: YOUR BEST EXAMPLE

For the second paragraph, pick your best example and use it to write a single paragraph that supports your position. Structure the paragraph as follows:

» **First sentence:** Present that example and mention that it supports your position as stated in the introduction.

» **Next several sentences:** Describe your example in greater detail.

» **Next sentence or two:** Show how your example supports your position as stated in the introduction.

» **Last sentence:** State unequivocally that the example you just presented clearly supports your position or refutes the counterargument.

TIP

Make sure one sentence (preferably the last sentence) of each paragraph connects back to your thesis in the introduction. This assures the evaluator that you're on track and your thoughts are organized. Check out the following example and compare it to the preceding list to see how I structured this second paragraph.

A wristwatch is a perfect example of a product that is better when mass-produced. My Casio watch was mass-produced with probably 10,000 other identical units. I purchased this watch five years ago, and it has consistently worked perfectly, with the occasional interruption for a battery replacement. The quality is fine, and the precision couldn't be better. Contrast this with my uncle's Patek Philippe, which was handmade with maybe a dozen others. Due to the motion-generated winding feature, his watch stops working when he doesn't wear it for more than two days! Clearly, this is neither precise timekeeping nor quality of utility. At any given moment, the Casio will always show the correct time, while the Patek's precision is a coin toss. The claim that mass-produced products lack the precision and quality of handmade goods, in this commonly occurring context, is clearly wrong.

Your examples don't need to be 100 percent correct. They serve to demonstrate how your powers of observation and insight support your point. The evaluators understand that you can't research anything while writing the essay. However, don't create examples out of thin air because they're likely to sound phony.

REMEMBER

WARNING

A clever writing style, as in describing the Patek's accuracy as "a coin toss," is encouraged. Again, though, be appropriate.

Make sure your examples aren't easily refutable. For example, if you're claiming that mass-produced goods are both better and cheaper, don't compare your mass-produced, affordable 4Runner to your great-grandfather's hand-built, now-priceless Model T. In this case, the 100 years of improved technology, not the method of production, is clearly the reason for the Toyota's superior performance and reliability. This comparison is a poor example because it's too easily refuted.

THIRD AND FOURTH PARAGRAPHS: YOUR NEXT BEST EXAMPLES

The third and fourth paragraphs of your essay are similar to the second paragraph. Each presents a single supporting example from your notes, shows how the example supports your position, and refers back to the introduction.

> However, some products, such as gentlemen's suits, are better as handmade items than as mass-produced commodities. For example, I wore an off-the-rack two-piece suit to my high school graduation. The jacket was slightly large, but the next size smaller was too small. The workmanship was mediocre, with loose threads and a misplaced stitch. It wasn't cheap, but it was mass-produced, and thus had neither quality nor precision. Contrast this with the handmade, professionally tailored suit that I bought last year. The precise fit is flawless and the quality is unparalleled. Though the claim that mass-produced products lack the quality and precision of handmade goods is true in this example, the claim still cannot be applied to all products.

Here's another example paragraph:

> Furthermore, some products can feature high or low quality and precision regardless of whether they are mass-produced or handmade. Computers are a good example of this. My mass-produced HP laptop demonstrates both precision and quality, while the Compaq computer I bought in 2016 lacked the quality to last more than 18 months. On the other hand, my friend hand-built a computer from parts ordered online, and his computer works with extremely high quality and precision. I have heard stories, however, of hand-built computers that didn't fare as well. Therefore, the general claim that mass-produced products lack the quality and precision of handmade goods is clearly flawed, because in this case, whether the product is handmade or mass-produced doesn't determine the outcome.

TIP

You don't need to always take *one* side of the issue. These examples of the wristwatch, gentlemen's suit, and computer clearly show different sides of the issue. However, the examples are consistent with the thesis, which is that a general claim of precision and quality cannot be applied to everything.

FINAL PARAGRAPH: THE CONCLUSION

Think of the final paragraph, the conclusion, as the closing bracket of your essay, with the introduction as the opening bracket. Your conclusion should mirror your introduction while leaving the evaluator with a sense of closure. Structure your concluding paragraph as follows:

> » **First sentence:** Restate your position on the issue presented in the prompt.
>
> » **Middle sentence or two:** Remind the reader of the supporting details and/or examples you presented and the logical conclusion those details and examples support.
>
> » **Final sentence:** Summarize why you agree or disagree with the issue statement presented on the test, and touch upon or restate your thesis statement.

TIP

You can refer to the introduction when you write the conclusion. They basically say the same thing, but the conclusion should be more robust because now you've explored the topic.

The following conclusion demonstrates how to follow these instructions:

> To sum up, one cannot correctly claim that all mass-produced products are inferior to handmade goods. The examples describing the wristwatch, the gentlemen's suit, and the personal computer clearly demonstrate that the claim may or may not be true, depending on the context and product. A claim that is sometimes true and sometimes not is an invalid claim, and this statement implies that it is always true. For this reason, I disagree with the statement, and I contend that some, but not all, mass-produced goods have better quality and precision than hand-built, carefully crafted products.

Exploring a sample essay

TIME: 30 minutes

Because society is always changing, laws should always change to reflect the times and be open to interpretation based on the facts of the individual circumstance.

DIRECTIONS: Write an essay in response to the preceding statement in which you discuss the extent to which you agree or disagree with the statement. Explain your reasoning in a clear, well-organized essay that supports your position. Consider both sides of the issue when developing your response.

Pause reading here and go type your practice essay. Then, check your notes and outline against the following information and insights. In this section, I present various ways to formulate and support a position in response to this essay prompt.

Having trouble getting started? Begin by identifying some relevant examples

If you had trouble getting started, maybe you couldn't think of any examples to write about. This particular essay prompt is on laws that change and those that should be flexible (open to interpretation), so start by jotting down some examples of laws that meet those criteria.

Here are examples of laws that changed in response to the changing times:

» New laws for new situations, such as cyberbullying laws today, DUI laws 50 years ago, and driver's license requirements 80 years ago

» Evolving laws for evolving situations, such as the use of marijuana

» Laws as a response to an event, such as terrorism or social media hacking

Examples of laws that may be flexible or open to interpretation include the following:

» Outdated and irrelevant laws, such as no carrying goldfish in Philadelphia or no dancing on Sundays

» Laws that justify killing, as in cases of self-defense or prevention of a tragedy

» Laws that address censorship and free speech

And because the prompt specifically instructs you to consider both sides of the issue, you need to think about laws that perhaps shouldn't change over time or be open to interpretation, such as laws prohibiting:

>> Murder or assassination

>> Assault and battery

>> Burglary

>> Vandalism

>> Hate crimes

Don't worry if some listed items wouldn't fit the essay — this is just a brain dump, and you don't have time to write on all of them anyway. When writing your essay, just pick the best few.

WARNING

Don't use examples that are out of scope, including the enforcement of laws, punishment, and regional differences. Also, avoid any hard-line stand on a politically charged topic.

Understanding how the essay is scored

Here are basic evaluator descriptions associated with each essay score:

>> **Outstanding (6):** The essay demonstrates your ability to take a position on a topic, support personal views and insights, and write with clarity, focus, and interest — in other words, you don't sound bored. The essay may have a grammar or spelling error but otherwise is well-written with control of the language, good *diction* (word choice), and variety of sentence structure.

>> **Strong (5):** The essay demonstrates your thoughtful analysis of the issue. Presentation is logical, and main points are well-supported. The essay may have minor errors in grammar and spelling but demonstrates control of the language, good diction, and variety of sentence structure.

>> **Adequate (4):** The essay demonstrates your overall competence in analyzing the issue, along with organizing and supporting your thoughts and expressing them clearly. It may not flow smoothly due to a lack of effective transitions, and it may contain some errors, but it demonstrates sufficient control of the language.

>> **Limited (3):** Competent but flawed, the essay (not yours, of course — someone else's) presents the issue poorly, lacks order, offers little or no support for the ideas presented, and contains occasional glaring errors or lots of minor errors in grammar, diction, and mechanics.

>> **Seriously flawed (2):** This person's essay completely misses the point, presents the author's point of view with no support or irrelevant support, is poorly organized, and has plenty of errors in grammar, word use, mechanics, and sentence construction.

>> **Fundamentally deficient (1):** The essay demonstrates little or no evidence of the author's ability to understand or analyze the issue. In addition, the essay contains extensive errors in grammar, word use, mechanics, and sentence structure.

>> **No essay (0):** The essay is blank or only garbage is typed in.

Sample essay — score 6 (outstanding)

Though laws should evolve and have some flexibility, I don't agree with the statement that laws should always change and be interpreted by each individual circumstance. Throughout history, laws have existed and evolved with society. Our laws today are based on a balance of rigidity and flexibility. There is always some adjustment and some interpretation, but to take away the foundation of the laws and leave them completely open to popularity and interpretation would lead us either to a libertine or totalitarian society, neither of which is healthy. In this essay, I will discuss laws that should evolve to keep pace with the new technology of an evolving society, especially regarding computers and cars. I will also discuss laws that should not be interpreted, such as premeditated murder, and finally laws that are no longer relevant and should possibly be scrubbed, such as how to carry goldfish. Though these are all valid topics for discussion, they do not suggest that all of our laws should be subject to interpretation and flexibility.

There are plenty of examples of laws that evolve with society out of necessity. Cyberbullying wasn't an issue 40 years ago, so there wouldn't be a law regarding this. Today, however, the framework for cyberbullying is in place, so the law exists out of necessity. When cars first came out, there were no laws requiring drivers' licenses or preventing drunk driving. The road was probably a very dangerous place! To keep up with a changing society, laws were introduced to regulate the road. Whether these laws are overreaching is another discussion, but overall the roads are safer with these laws than without them. In these cases — cyberbullying and roads — the laws are changing to reflect the times, and this is good.

However, these changes should be careful and deliberate. Other laws, such as prohibiting premeditated murder, cannot simply be flexible or interpreted based on circumstance. Around 1995, the Israeli prime minister Yitzchak Rabin was assassinated days before signing a peace treaty with Yasser Arafat, the leader of the PLO. The assassin was not a criminal before this, but he felt that the provision of the treaty would have placed the Israeli people in danger, and this was his motive for murder. His rationale was to kill one person to save many. Whether he was right is a topic for debate, but for the purpose of this essay, let's suppose that yes: the treaty would have led to the deaths of many Israelis. Was his act justified? This is the danger of leaving laws to interpretation. If you say that yes, in this case, it was justified, then it basically opens the door to quite a lawless society. The law against murder becomes null, because there's always a circumstance and interpretation making it OK. Our CEO is leading the company to bankruptcy. Kill her! My neighbor parties all night and keeps me up, so I may lose my job. Kill him! This is absolutely NOT the direction that things should go. Laws like this, prohibiting premeditated murder and certain other crimes, should not be open to flexibility and interpretation, and Rabin's assassin was rightly prosecuted in spite of his lofty motive.

There are also laws that have faded to irrelevancy and are no longer enforced, but this is not the same as interpretation or circumstantial allowance. For example, "It's illegal to walk on the sidewalks of Philadelphia carrying goldfish," or "It is a crime to sing to your horses in the hearing of others" are examples of laws that are no longer relevant. I have always wondered what would happen if one of these obscure laws were suddenly enforced again. Can you imagine walking out of a pet store on a Sunday afternoon with a goldfish and getting busted? Legally, law enforcement could do this — it's the law. Fortunately, they don't, but it brings up the point that as laws become irrelevant or obsolete, they may require some review. However, this is not the same as interpreting or making exceptions. These are laws that are obsolete because society has evolved away from them.

Laws should evolve and have some flexibility, but not too much. New technology, such as cars and computers, require new laws. Some old, obsolete laws probably have no place anymore in our modern society. However, certain laws cannot be flexible, such as killing one person to save many.

Evaluator comments on the score 6 essay

This essay presents an excellent answer to the question. The writer uses powerful, relevant examples to support his point and makes the clear case that though some flexibility and interpretation is warranted, it has to be controlled.

The writer's opinion is clear from the start and is supported by well-reasoned and thoroughly developed examples. Though the thesis is not blatantly declared, the author's position is clearly stated in the first paragraph and reinforced by the following paragraphs. The three examples are separated, yet they flow together well via the use of good transitions. The ending sums things up nicely and leaves no doubt as to the author's opinion.

TIP

Your examples are more powerful if they're relevant to real life. Also, the evaluators know that you're not able to do research while taking the GRE, so it's okay if you're not sure of a detail, such as the year something happened or who exactly said a certain quote. The evaluators are simply interested in whether you can make a point and support it well.

Sample essay — score 4 (adequate)

Laws must change when Society changes. This is true for all types of laws, the major laws and the minor laws. This is true for all types of Societies, the so-called First World and lesser developed countries. This is true for all types of situations, from the serious to the silly to the macabre.

An example of when a law must change is the death penalty. Many years ago, condemned prisoners were executed routinely. Such executions became major events, almost parties, with the public making an excursion to watch the hanging. The irony, of course, is that the huge crowds at the execution attracted additional criminals who then committed more crimes (theft, pickpocketing, assault) and perpetated the cycle. Today, while there are less executions, they have become media events. We don't attend the executions in person, but we live through them vicariously, watching them on tv. When Timothy McVeigh, the Oklahoma City bomber, was given a lethal injection, the tv stations carried a minute-by-minute report. The amount of money and time and energy that was put into this could have been better spent elsewhere.

A second reason laws must be flexible is in time of war or social upheaval. Take, for example, the 1960's. The United States had a sea of change during that decade. Many more things were acceptable socially then than had ever been before, and the laws had to change to reflect that fact. The possession of certain drugs became much less serious than it had been before. People weren't sentenced to twenty years for *using* drugs, just for *pushing* them. Today, people can use certain drugs legally, either recreationally or for medicinal purposes depending on the state where they live.

Traffic laws are a less serious, but still good, example of when laws should change. The speed limit in downtown New York must obviously be less than that in the outskirts of Podunk, Idaho (my apologies to the Podunkians!). Many people in Wyoming and other sparsely-populated Western states fought against having a federally-mandated speed limit of 55 on the freeways, rguing that in their areas, 65 or even 75 would be more logical. This is an example of the need for a change to meet the needs of a local community or Society. The same is true for the age at which youngsters can get a license, as they are more mature earlier now than before.

In conclusion, laws are not static because people are not static. We change from decade to decade, and from locale to locale. While it is important to adhere to the Declaration of Independence's statement that "all [people] are created equal," and thus should have equal rights, not all times are created equal, and thus should not have equal laws.

Evaluator comments on the score 4 essay

This is a generally acceptable response. The writer presents an unequivocal answer to the question and uses some good vocabulary ("macabre," "vicariously"). In addition, the length is good, with three well-organized examples.

However, the examples are out of scope. The money, time, and energy spent watching McVeigh's execution isn't relevant to changing laws. It's not clear why wars and social upheavals mandate a change in laws, or during which times the laws or the enforcement changed. And the speed limit differences in differently populated areas aren't shown to have changed; they are shown to be different.

The essay has additional weaknesses that prevent it from receiving a higher score, such as instances of inappropriate humor ("my apologies to the Podunkians!"). Although minor grammatical flaws are acceptable, "less executions" should be "fewer executions" and therefore isn't acceptable. Though an occasional typo and spelling or capitalization error is acceptable, this essay has far too many, such as *perpetated* instead of *perpetuated*, *tv* instead of *TV* or *television*, *rguing* instead of *arguing*, and *Society* instead of *society*.

Preparing for the Verbal Section

It's time to brush up on your English. That's a *lot* to cover — you can get a college degree in English. But, for the purposes of this test, where do you start? How far do you go?

Fortunately, GRE Verbal is based on a specific set of skills that, with this book, you can identify and build. You don't need outside knowledge of any particular topic except for vocabulary, and even that can be augmented through skills and learning rather than rote memorization.

Building your core skills

Most GRE Verbal questions are based on your comprehension and critical thinking skills from reading at a college level. If you can read — and truly understand — a scientific or business journal piece, along with its vocabulary, then you're well on your way to achieving a good Verbal score.

If you don't regularly read college-level pieces — and who does? — then you should start now. For business, read a few pieces from *The Economist* or *The Financial Times;* for science, visit the List of Scientific Journals in Wikipedia and find some topics that you're interested in, or, better yet, are in your field of study for your upcoming master's program. The harder to read, the better.

Why would you do this? GRE Verbal isn't specific to any topic, and any detail that you need is included with the question. It's because most of GRE Verbal consists of *esoteric* (not understood by most) writing of concepts and passages that the exam expects you to handle with ease, and most people can't *access* (understand) without practice. This is why few test-takers score well on GRE Verbal, and why this section is so challenging on the GRE.

As you read these college-level journal pieces, make sure that you understand each paragraph. Don't just gloss over something that's not clear. You'll have a master's or PhD at this level soon enough, so this piece should be something that you can read and understand. Then — and here's why this is relevant — when you take the GRE, the Verbal section isn't such a challenge.

This approach even builds up your vocabulary. As you read these pieces, look up any word that you don't know. Eventually, you'll see these words repeated, and you'll also see them in GRE Verbal. You don't need a dictionary or web browser. Just tap on your phone or say, "Hey, Alexa (or Google or Siri), what is *loquacious*?" (It means talkative.)

We review 20 vocab words at the start of each GRE class. One time, a student brought in a *New York Times* article that had three of the words from the last class! She said that she never even noticed those words before we had reviewed them. The takeaway for you: Don't let a *single* word go by without looking up and understanding its meaning.

Clinching text completion and sentence equivalence questions

Text Completion and Sentence Equivalence questions are similar but have some distinct differences:

REMEMBER

>> **Text Completion:** A Text Completion question consists of a sentence or paragraph with one, two, or three missing words or phrases, along with a short list of word or phrase choices to complete the text. If the text has one word missing, the list has five choices, while if the text has two or three words missing, each blank has a list of three choices.

Each choice gives the text a different meaning. Your job is to choose the word or words that best support the meaning of the sentence. If the text is missing more than one word, you don't get partial credit for choosing only one correct word.

Text Completion questions tend to have slightly easier vocabulary but are more challenging to interpret.

>> **Sentence Equivalence:** A Sentence Equivalence question consists of a single sentence with exactly one word missing and a list of six choices to complete it. Your job is to select the two words that fit the sentence *and* mean the same thing, and, as with the Text Completion questions, you don't get partial credit for choosing only one correct word.

TIP

Sentence Completion questions tend to be easier to interpret but have more challenging vocabulary. The correct answers are *almost always* synonyms. If you find a word that works well but doesn't have a match, then you've likely found a *trap answer*.

>> **Both question types:** The answer choices always fit perfectly and have perfect grammar: Make your choice based on the *meaning* of the words. Each word you place gives the sentence a different meaning, so find the meaning of the text *without* the answer choices, and then eliminate the wrong answer choices.

Keeping it straight

Don't worry about memorizing how many answers to click. On the exam it's clear, and just to be sure, at the top of the screen is always an instruction that reads something like "Pick one answer for each missing word (in Text Completion)" or "Pick two answer choices that create sentences most alike in meaning (in Sentence Equivalence)."

Also, the one-answer questions allow you to select only one answer, and the two-answer questions allow you to select more than one. Go through it once and you'll be fine: I've never had a student mix this up.

Developing your skills for finding the correct answers

Text Completion and Sentence Equivalence questions are designed to measure two core proficiencies: interpreting the text and using the vocabulary. These are two distinct skills that you build separately but use together. The following two sections provide tips on each skill.

REMEMBER

Most of the vocab words that you encounter on the GRE are used commonly in most professional industries, including business and journalism. Such words as *ephemeral* (fleeting), *abscond* (sneak away), and *imbroglio* (entanglement) stump exam-takers every day but appear regularly in publications.

INTERPRETING THE TEXT 101

Interpreting the text means discerning its meaning in the absence of key words. Do this prior to looking at the answer choices to understand the text and quickly eliminate choices that don't make sense. Try this simple example:

Directions: Select the two answer choices that, when used to complete the sentence, fit the meaning as a whole and produce two completed sentences that are alike in meaning.

PLAY

The boxes were so heavy that we could _____ lift them.

(A) easily

(B) hardly

(C) fully

(D) nearly

(E) barely

(F) effortlessly

Even without the missing word, you can construe the meaning of the sentence. The phrase *so heavy* tells you that these boxes are difficult or impossible to lift. After realizing this, you can immediately eliminate *easily* and *effortlessly*. The words *fully* and *nearly* are a little tougher to ignore, but they really don't make sense either. The correct answers are Choices (B), *hardly*, and (E), *barely.*

GETTING THE GIST OF THE TEXT

One way to figure out the meaning of a challenging sentence is to see whether it has a positive or negative connotation. This high-level perspective can help you find words that convey the correct meaning. Try it out on this example. Though not really a tough sentence, it shows you what I mean:

Directions: Select the two answer choices that, when used to complete the sentence, fit the meaning of the sentence as a whole and produce two completed sentences that are alike in meaning.

PLAY

Everyone is so _____ that you did great on the GRE: We knew you could do it!

(A) ecstatic

(B) stunned

(C) thrilled

(D) shocked

(E) dumbfounded

(F) bewildered

All the choices suggest that you did better than expected, but *stunned, shocked, dumbfounded,* and *bewildered* imply that everyone thought you would tank, and what kind of friends are those? However, we knew you would do great, probably because you used *GRE 5-Hour Quick Prep For Dummies.* The second half of the sentence doesn't convey doubt ("We knew you could do it!"), so the correct answers are Choices (A) and (C).

Taking the Best and Only Approach

Whether you're taking on a Text Completion or Sentence Equivalence question, your approach is the same. These steps are the *only* way to knock out these questions so you can beat the exam and get on with your life.

1. Interpret the text without looking at the answer choices.

2. Complete the text with your own words.

3. Eliminate wrong answer choices.

Comprehending the reading questions

Reading Comprehension passages are typically based on either biological and physical sciences, social sciences, or humanities. They can also be the most time-consuming questions of the Verbal section. The best way to ace these questions is to master and use strategies for quickly reading the passages, identifying key facts called for in the questions, and drawing inferences based on subtle implications. Ask yourself the purpose of the passage: Why is the author writing this? The following sections explain four useful strategies for effectively and efficiently arriving at the correct answers (and avoiding incorrect answers).

TIP

The best way to master reading comprehension — meaning you can read the passage quickly and understand it on all its levels — is through *practice.* Make these graduate-level paragraphs something you read before breakfast, not something you force yourself through every few weeks. They don't have to be GRE examples, but mobile clips from Facebook and LinkedIn don't bring your reading skills up to par. Instead, practice reading *The Economist, Financial Times, Wall Street Journal, New Yorker,* or any number of intellectual publications on a topic you're interested in, maybe even in your field of study.

Using the context as your road map

Read the passage lightly and get a general idea of where the key information is and what is going on in the passage. This helps you figure out where to find the information as you begin to answer questions. *Remember:* Don't sweat the details (yet). After reading a question, you can quickly revisit the passage to locate the details for answering the question correctly.

TIP

Usually, the first paragraph or sentence and/or the last paragraph or sentence tells you what the passage is about (the main idea). The rest of the passage supports or develops this idea. As you read each body paragraph, pay attention to its purpose and how it supports the main idea. This is a key strategy to understanding the passage, and it becomes almost a habit with practice.

REMEMBER

Sometimes the entire passage is one giant paragraph. Don't let that deter you from using this strategy. Look for where one idea ends and another begins and treat that as where the paragraphs should be separated. This can help you map the details as you would for a passage that is actually in separate paragraphs.

Grasping the gist of the passage

Understanding the main idea of the passage is the key to establishing the context of the paragraphs within. The main idea is typically the basis of one of the questions. If you can briefly sum up *why* the author is writing the passage, then you've not only developed a contextual understanding of the passage, but also answered one of the questions ahead of time.

Avoiding common traps

The folks who write the GRE are a tricky lot. They bait you with wrong but tempting answers, hoping you'll bite. By recognizing these common traps, you have a better chance of avoiding them. Here are a few to watch out for:

>> **Mixing the main idea with details:** Questions asking the main idea or primary purpose of the passage have answer choices that are true but aren't the main idea. These are trap answers. For example, a passage may describe light pollution from cars or streetlights that obscures stars at night. The main idea isn't the car headlights or streetlights: It's the overall effect on nighttime visibility.

Double-check the first and last sentences. Is the author asking for increased funding or a course of action? Is the passage challenging a common notion? If you know *why* the author is writing this, you'll know the primary purpose of the passage and not be distracted by detail answers.

One strategy is to work main idea or primary purpose questions last, especially with a long Reading Comprehension passage. Because you can go back and forth through the questions, you can work them in any order. As you answer the detail questions, you learn more about the main idea; then you can go back and answer that main idea question. Just don't *forget* it and move forward, leaving that question unanswered.

>> **Mixing cause-and-effect relationships:** Answer choices typically mix up the cause-and-effect relationships of details in the passage. If the tide comes in because of the moon, for example, and this causes all the ships to rise, the question will check your understanding of what caused what to happen.

Skim the passage for key words relating to the cause-and-effect described in the question. From the preceding example, look for the words *moon, tide,* and *ships.* Find the discussion of these events, and make sure the answer choice reflects the events discussed in the passage.

>> **Mixing in your own knowledge:** You may know something about the topic at hand. If you're like most people, you add detail based on your own knowledge and expertise from other things that you've read. Sometimes, these details tempt you to choose an answer that's true by your understanding but wrong per the passage. Be careful not to mix your own knowledge with what's in the passage.

I had a student who was a chemistry major work on a Reading Comp passage on chemistry, and she vehemently disagreed with what was in the passage. She was probably right — but she got all the questions wrong, based on what she *thought* it should be instead of what the passage said.

If you're familiar with the topic, that's a good thing: You'll understand the passage better than the other test-takers. However, the passage may take a break from reality, so just take what it says with a grain of salt. Note the differences, but don't challenge the passage. Instead, go along with its fantasy story and get all the questions right.

Answering the question yourself

One good way to dodge the answer-choice traps is to answer the question yourself first, before looking at the answer choices. Get a sense of what the right answer *should be*, then eliminate the wrong answer choices.

The right answer won't match your own answer. That's okay, it doesn't have to. What it does is make the *wrong* answers clearly stand out, so that you can take them out of the running and focus on what remains. With a sense of what the right answer *should* be, four answers will stand out as *not a chance* and one will stand out as *maybe*. Go with the *maybe:* You can always return to it later.

WARNING

Don't change your own answer based on the answer choices! Don't think, "maybe it's *that.*" I've had students do this, and it defeats the whole strategy. You're sharp, you get it, you know what the answer choice should look like — so trust yourself! Besides, four of the answer choices are dead wrong, so why would you change your own answer to match one of those?

Thinking through argument analysis questions

An *Argument Analysis* question asks you to determine what new fact strengthens, weakens, or completes the argument, along with some variations. This section shows you what to look for in the argument and how to approach the question and answer choices that follow it — a useful skill in day-to-day life, but this section is geared specifically toward the GRE take.

Use this five-step approach to take on an Argument Analysis question:

1. **Cover the answer choices.**

2. **Read the question for what it's asking.**

3. **Read the passage for what the question is asking.**

4. **Answer the question in your own words.**

5. **Eliminate each wrong answer.**

This section leads you through this five-step process and either transforms you into a critical thinker or makes you more of one.

Covering the answer choices

First, don't look at the answer choices. Avoiding the choices *facilitates* (eases) your ability to follow the argument, because all but one of the answer choices are wrong, and they clutter your brain with *superfluous* (nonessential) and *equivocal* (misleading) information. The wrong answer choices try to distract you, so don't let them. Instead, cover them with your hand or scratch paper.

Reading the question for what it's asking

Still covering the answer choices, read and understand the question so you know what to look for in the passage. The question typically asks you which answer choice does one of the following:

>> Most seriously weakens the argument

>> Best supports the argument

>> Draws the most reasonable conclusion from the argument

>> Identifies the assumption that must be true for the argument to be true

>> Most accurately represents the premise on which the argument is based

The questions may not use the actual wording provided here; for example, instead of asking which choice most seriously *weakens* the argument, a question may ask which choice most effectively *undermines* (weakens) the argument. Don't get hung up on the wording — just be sure to understand what the question is looking for.

Reading the passage for what the question is asking

Now, knowing what the question is looking for, you're better equipped to *actively read* — read with a purpose. Instead of just reading the words, ask yourself critical questions, such as "How is the conclusion drawn?" "What would strengthen this argument?" "What would weaken this argument?" and "What's the author assuming?"

Having read the question first, you can take this critical reading step because you know what to look for. The active reading is guided, because the exam gives you the *one* question to answer, and you read it before reading the argument.

The following sections provide guidance on what to look for in a passage when answering different types of Argument Analysis questions.

IDENTIFYING THE "BECAUSE" AND "THEREFORE"

Think of a logical argument as an if-then statement, where *because* of a certain set of facts, *therefore* you will have this result or plan. When reading an argument, break it down into these two parts:

>> **Because:** The *because* (the *if* part) is facts or reasons that support the therefore, including observations, statistics, reasonable generalizations, and anecdotes.

>> **Therefore:** The *therefore* (the *then* part), which is the result of the because, is the argument's main point, plan, or assertion.

After identifying the *because* and *therefore*, you have what you need to begin your argument analysis, as I explain in the next few sections. Consider this simple argument:

Our dog Rover came in from the backyard, and the flower bed is all dug up! Rover must have dug up the flower bed.

To analyze this argument, place it in the *because/therefore* template. You can paraphrase the argument:

>> **Because** Rover was in the backyard,

>> **Therefore** he dug up the flower bed.

This single, simple restatement of the argument helps you evaluate the answer choices without having to reread the entire passage.

TIP

Look for the following words to identify the conclusion: *then, therefore, thus, hence, so, consequently, as a result, must have,* and *in conclusion.* However, don't rely solely on these words; they may be implied rather than stated.

However, this simple argument is flawed. You could *weaken* it by introducing new evidence that suggests Rover *didn't* dig up the flower bed. You could also *strengthen* it by introducing new evidence that suggests he *did* dig up the bed.

Start with the *assumption* of the argument, which isn't stated in the passage. What do you think the assumption is? That no other kids or dogs were in the yard, leaving Rover responsible. I discuss finding this further in the next section.

What new evidence *weakens* the argument? Rover wasn't alone in the backyard — Ginger (the neighbor's dog) and the kids were also in the backyard! In this case, Rover *may* have dug up the flower garden, or he may not have. You *can't* be sure.

What new evidence *strengthens* the argument? Rover *was* alone in the backyard — no other dogs or kids (or anything else that tends to dig). In this case, Rover *must* have dug up the yard, because there's no other plausible explanation. You *can* be sure.

Whether you introduce new evidence that *weakens* or *strengthens* the argument depends on what the question asks. With a longer, more complicated argument, it really helps if you know what you're trying to do as you read the passage — and this is why you read the question first!

FINDING THE UNSTATED ASSUMPTION

An *assumption* is a claim that the passage makes without stating it directly. The assumption is based on the *because* part and suggests that the argument has only one reasonable conclusion. When asked to identify an assumption, think of what *must* be true for the argument to work. This is the part that isn't *stated* in the passage, so it takes some critical thinking.

> Employees in the sales department had special training, and now they perform better than they did before. This special training should thus be given to the employees in all other departments to improve their performance also.

Like many arguments, this argument has more than one *because* and *therefore*, each with its own unstated assumption.

First because and therefore in this argument

>> **Because** sales employees had special training,

>> **Therefore** they now perform better.

Between this first *because* and the *therefore* is the unstated assumption that the improved performance in the sales department is a direct result of the special training. What is the assumption? That nothing else happened that improved their performance.

To *strengthen* or *weaken* the argument, go for the assumption. You could *weaken* it by introducing new evidence that suggests the training *didn't* improve the sales employees' performance. You could also *strengthen* it by introducing new evidence that suggests it *did* improve the performance.

What new evidence *weakens* the argument? A lot of things would work: The salespeople were novices, and they learned on the job. They got new leadership. They got lots of new leads. The product went down in price and improved in quality. The competition went out of business. The demand increased, for whatever reason. You get the point — the performance improvement may not have been a result of the special training.

What new evidence *strengthens* the argument? That none of these previously mentioned factors changed: The leadership, leads, product, competition, and demand *didn't* change. In this case, the improved performance probably was from the special training.

Second because and therefore in this argument

>> **Because** sales employees had special training and now perform better,

>> **Therefore** this special training should be given to the other employees so they also perform better.

Between this second *because* and the *therefore* is the unstated assumption that the training that is effective for the sales department will also be effective for the other departments. What is the assumption? That the training is universally effective.

To *strengthen* or *weaken* the argument at this point, go for this assumption. You could *weaken* it by introducing new evidence that suggests the training *only* affects the sales department. You could *strengthen* it by introducing new evidence that suggests that the training is beneficial for *all* departments.

What new evidence *weakens* the argument? You could make it about the special training — it's specific to sales; it fits the salesperson demographic; it addresses anything specific to the sales department. In other words, this training *wouldn't* have much of an effect on the other departments.

What new evidence *strengthens* the argument? Basically the opposite of what weakens it: The special training is for general employee skills; it's effective for all demographics and job types; basically it's *not* specific to sales. In this case, the special training *would* help other departments.

For this plan to work, both assumptions must be true. You don't need to think about them to the level described previously, and typically the answer choices mention *one* assumption — but now you know what to look for and how to critically approach an argument or plan.

TIP

Writing the Analyze an Argument essay is *exactly* like this — only instead of answering a question, you write an essay. Basically, each paragraph covers one assumption.

EXPLORING COMMON LOGICAL FALLACIES

Arguments may seem logical and fair on the surface but actually be *fallacious* (erroneous, flawed). The following sections reveal some of the more common logical fallacies you're likely to find on the exam. By spotting these, you identify weaknesses in arguments and gather the knowledge required to determine which statements best support or refute the argument.

>> **Erroneous cause-and-effect:** An erroneous cause-and-effect assumes that because two events happened, one must have caused the other. For example — true story — a study came out saying that taking selfies makes you more confident. How did these brilliant researchers arrive at such a profound conclusion? Apparently, people who take lots of selfies are more confident — so it must be that the selfies bring confidence. What do you think of this? Personally, I think that people take selfies *because* they're confident, not the other way around.

>> **Sweeping generalization:** A *sweeping generalization* applies a general rule to a specific case. It suggests that a plan that works in one context will work in another. For example, because the addition of sharp-turn warning signs to roads in Town *X* reduced the rate of accidents, adding these signs to the roads in Town *Y* will surely have the same effect. This argument uses a sweeping generalization by assuming that the roads in the two towns are similar. However, is it possible that the two towns are different? It could be that Town *X* has lots of curvy mountain roads, while Town *Y* has only straight, flat roads. Because sharp-turn warning signs don't make straight roads safer, the addition of these signs to roads in Town *Y* will not have the intended effect.

> » **Misplaced motive:** A *misplaced motive* assumes that someone did something on purpose when really that person didn't have an option. For example, if the play director is selecting students to act in the high-school play, and the director comes back with a list of only seniors, the assumption may be that the director has a motive to work with seniors, for whatever reason: They're experienced, mature, taller, afflicted with senioritis, or any other reason. Is it possible that the director had no such motive? It could be that only seniors applied to act in the play — no juniors, sophomores, or freshmen wanted to participate — so the director only had seniors to choose from. It wasn't the director's motive at all: It was just the limited options.

REMEMBER

Of course, these logical fallacies are just broad categories. GRE Argument Analysis fallacies include these but also can be more varied and specific — but looking for these common fallacies helps you get started in critically approaching the Argument passages. If you don't see one of these example fallacies, you'll probably find something *else* that you can use to strengthen or weaken the argument.

Answering the question in your own words

After you have a clear understanding of the argument's premise and conclusion, which make up the Because and Therefore, and you've identified the assumption that the argument hinges upon, answer the question in your own words. For one thing, this gives the wrong answer choices less power to lead you astray. Use the question as your focal point. For example, if the question asks you to weaken the argument, you can use the skills you just learned to identify the assumption and think of new evidence that weakens the assumption.

Following are the different question types and what you need to ask yourself and answer before looking at the answer choices:

> » **Weakening the plan or argument:** What new information that's not in the plan or argument would weaken it? Does the argument commit a logical fallacy? If so, which one?
>
> » **Strengthening the plan argument:** What new information that's not in the plan or argument would strengthen it? It could be that there's no other relevant information, so the assumption is probably true.
>
> » **Identifying the assumption:** What assumption does the plan or argument hinge on that, if proven untrue, would render the conclusion false?

WARNING

Be sure to stay away from the answer choices until you've answered the question in your own words. Even though the right answer is in there, there are also four wrong answers designed to distract and mislead you.

Eliminating each wrong answer

After you've answered the question in your own words, the next step is to eliminate wrong answer choices. Your answer won't match the correct answer, but it doesn't have to. The purpose of answering the question yourself is less to get a sense of what the correct answer looks like and more to make the clearly wrong answers stand out, so that you can eliminate them.

WARNING

Avoid the trap that I've seen too many students fall into. *Don't change your own answer based on the answer choices!* Four of the answer choices are wrong, and changing your answer defeats the whole strategy. Even if your own answer is wrong, it'll be close enough for you to spot and eliminate the wrong answers.

This strategy is relevant to most of the Verbal questions on the GRE — eliminating the obviously wrong answers and working with what's left. The following sections show you how to eliminate wrong answers and highlight some common traps to avoid.

APPLYING THE PROCESS OF ELIMINATION

GRE developers take pleasure in intentionally misleading you, the test-taker. To defend yourself against this underhanded *chicanery* (deceit), brush up on these common traps.

BEWARE OF "SOME"

If an argument applies a sweeping generalization, it's understood that the generalization may not apply to the entire population. For example, if the argument is to reduce jaywalking by issuing tickets, and the question asks you to weaken the argument, a trap answer would read, "Some jaywalkers don't care about paying the tickets." This may be true, but *most* jaywalkers *do* care about paying tickets, and the argument/plan would still reduce jaywalking even if some jaywalkers don't care.

STAY IN SCOPE

A trap answer choice may contain information that's irrelevant to the argument. For example, if the argument is that dolphins absorb too much mercury because they eat too much fish, and the question asks you to weaken the argument, a trap answer would be that seals also eat too much fish but don't absorb mercury. Whether you're strengthening or weakening this argument, you can eliminate this answer choice, because whatever happens with seals is out of scope of dolphins.

DON'T GO WITH AN ANSWER JUST BECAUSE IT'S TRUE

The correct answer will be true, but a trap answer is also true — so make sure it answers the question. In the preceding two examples, the sample trap answers, "Some jaywalkers don't care about paying the tickets" and "Seals also eat too much fish," are certainly true — but they don't answer the question, so they're wrong.

DON'T BE TEMPTED BY OPPOSITES

If you're asked to weaken or support the argument, the answer choices almost always contain at least one statement that does the exact opposite. It may make sense because it contains the elements that you're looking for, but make sure it goes in the right direction. If you're strengthening an argument, for example, this trap answer will fit perfectly but actually weaken the argument.

Exploring sample questions

Now that you're familiar with the questions types on the Verbal sections, work through these sample questions to check your understanding. The explanations that follow each sample question enable you to check your answer and understand why the correct answer is right.

Text completion

PLAY

Directions: For each blank, select one entry from the corresponding column of choices. Fill all blanks in the way that best completes the text.

1. As a public relations specialist, Susan realizes the importance of treating even the most exasperating tourists with kindness and _____.

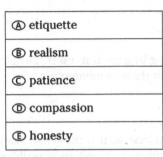

Ⓐ etiquette

Ⓑ realism

Ⓒ patience

Ⓓ compassion

Ⓔ honesty

First, ask yourself, "What's important when dealing with exasperated tourists?" A public relations specialist would need to be polite. The first word choice, *etiquette*, looks good, but you don't treat someone with etiquette. (*Etiquette* is a system of rules for manners.) Cross that word off the list. You don't show exasperating tourists *compassion*, either. Gone. *Honesty* won't help. Gone! *Realism* isn't even close. Gone! Through logic and elimination, or just because it's the only one remaining, the correct answer is Choice (C), *patience*.

2. Enabled by his (i) _____ and unimpeded by any sense of (ii) _____, Henry reached the end of the Ironman Triathlon.

Blank (i)	Blank (ii)
Ⓐ knowhow	Ⓓ weariness
Ⓑ appetite	Ⓔ courage
Ⓒ stamina	Ⓕ power

What's one thing that helps and another that hinders a triathlete? *Strength* and *fatigue* are good choices. In the first column, you can rule out *knowhow*. Either of the remaining words, *appetite* (in the sense of desire) and *stamina*, could fit, but stamina is more closely related to strength. In the second blank, eliminate words that don't match *fatigue*, and *weariness* is left over. Correct answers: Choices (C) and (D).

3. Although dismayed by the pejorative comments made about her inappropriate dress at the diplomatic function, Judy (i) _____ her tears and showed only the most calm and (ii) _____ visage to her critics.

Blank (i)	Blank (ii)
Ⓐ suppressed	Ⓓ incensed
Ⓑ monitored	Ⓔ articulate
Ⓒ succumbed to	Ⓕ placid

If Judy had a calm and (something) *visage* (a form of the word *vision*; a countenance, or facial expression), the (something) must go hand in hand with *calm*. Although the second word doesn't have to be an exact synonym, it can't be an antonym, either. Look for a word that means calm. *Placid* means calm and tranquil, from the root *plac*, meaning peace (as in *placate*). Check the remaining two choices in the second column: *Incensed* means burning mad (think of burning incense); *articulate* means well-spoken. Her visage (or facial expression) would not be well-spoken, although Judy herself may be, so cross off *articulate*. *Placid* is therefore best for the second word, so now find something suitable for the first word. *Monitoring* or *succumbing to* (giving in to) her tears is unlikely to make Judy appear calm and placid, but *suppressing* her tears will. The correct answers are Choices (A) and (F).

Sentence equivalence

PLAY

Directions: Select the two answer choices that, when used to complete the sentence, fit the meaning as a whole and produce two completed sentences that are alike in meaning.

1. A successful business-process _____ designed to streamline existing operations will, by its nature, also support the company's strategic planning.

   (A) reaction
   (B) management
   (C) innovation
   (D) initiative
   (E) supply chain
   (F) method

   Is this business-process thing a new event or ongoing? That it's designed to affect "existing operations" tells you that it doesn't currently exist and is therefore new. Look for words that suggest an early phase of development. *Reaction* obviously doesn't fit. *Management* and *supply chain* are business-sounding words that don't suggest anything new. *Method* also isn't distinctly new (a method could have been around for a while). The words *innovation* and *initiative* suggest something in the early stages of development. The correct answers are Choices (C) and (D).

2. The sea tortoise, though lumbering and slow on land, moves with _____ speed and agility in water.

   (A) surprising
   (B) actual
   (C) according
   (D) defiant
   (E) unexpected
   (F) unequivocal

   If the tortoise is lumbering and slow on land, wouldn't you expect it to be slow in water, too? The crocodile, for example, is fast and nimble in either environment (which can be bad news). In this sentence, however, the transition word *though* tells you that the tortoise's speed and agility in water is a surprise. The words *actual, according, defiant,* and *unequivocal* (straightforward) don't suggest any sort of surprise. The correct answers are Choices (A) and (E).

3. The speaker _____ the very point he had stood up to make and hurriedly sat down, hoping no one had caught his solecism.

   (A) prognosticated

   (B) divulged

   (C) refuted

   (D) countered

   (E) duplicated

   (F) ferreted out

A *solecism* is an inconsistency, such as a mistake. From the context of the sentence, you can gather that something negative happened because the speaker hoped no one had noticed it. Sounds like the speaker had contradicted himself. Now review and eliminate wrong answers:

To *prognosticate* is to predict, which is out. *Divulge,* meaning to reveal, is also out. To *ferret out* is to search diligently, and you know what *duplicate* is, both of which don't work, leaving *refute* (disprove) and *counter* (contradict), similar enough to produce sentences alike in meaning. The correct answers are Choices (C) and (D).

Reading

The following sample questions include the four types of reading passages you'll see on the GRE: biology and physical science, social science, humanities, and social science.

THE BIOLOGICAL AND PHYSICAL SCIENCE PASSAGE

A biological or physical science passage is straightforward, giving you the scoop on something. It may be how stellar dust is affected by gravity, how to build a suspension bridge, or how molecular theory applies. The passage may be difficult to get through (because it goes into depth on an unfamiliar subject), so read it quickly for the gist and go back later for the details.

REMEMBER

When approaching biological and physical science passages, don't get hung up on the scientific terminology. Just accept these terms as part of the story and keep reading. The terms may function as key words to help you locate the answers within the passage even if you don't know what the terms mean.

Here's a science passage for you to practice on. Don't forget to check the introduction paragraph for the overall gist of the passage and to look for the high-level contribution of each paragraph. If you know each paragraph's purpose, you can quickly find the details when you need them.

> Microbiological activity clearly affects the mechanical strength of leaves. Although it cannot be denied that with most species the loss of mechanical strength is the result of both invertebrate feeding and microbiological breakdown, the example of *Fagus sylvatica* illustrates loss without any sign of invertebrate attack being evident. *Fagus* shows little sign of invertebrate attack even after being exposed for eight months in either a lake or stream environment, but results of the rolling fragmentation experiment show that loss of mechanical strength, even in this apparently resistant species, is considerable.
>
> Most species appear to exhibit a higher rate of degradation in the stream environment than in the lake. This is perhaps most clearly shown in the case of *Alnus*. Examination of the type of destruction suggests that the cause for the greater loss of material in the stream-processed leaves is a

combination of both biological and mechanical degradation. The leaves exhibit an angular fragmentation, which is characteristic of mechanical damage, rather than the rounded holes typical of the attack by large particle feeders or the skeletal vein pattern produced by microbial degradation and small particle feeders. As the leaves become less strong, the fluid forces acting on the stream nylon cages cause successively greater fragmentation.

Mechanical fragmentation, like biological breakdown, is to some extent influenced by leaf structure and form. In some leaves with a strong midrib, the lamina breaks up, but the pieces remain attached by means of the midrib. One type of leaf may break cleanly, whereas another tears off and is easily destroyed after the tissues are weakened by microbial attack.

In most species, the mechanical breakdown will take the form of gradual attrition at the margins. If the energy of the environment is sufficiently high, brittle species may be broken across the midrib, something that rarely happens with more pliable leaves. The result of attrition is that where the areas of the whole leaves follow a normal distribution, a bimodal distribution is produced, one peak composed mainly of the fragmented pieces, the other of the larger remains.

To test the theory that a thin leaf has only half the chance of a thick one for entering the fossil record, all other things being equal, Ferguson (1971) cut discs of fresh leaves from 11 species of leaves, each with a different thickness, and rotated them with sand and water in a revolving drum. Each run lasted 100 hours and was repeated three times, but even after this treatment, all species showed little sign of wear. It therefore seems unlikely that leaf thickness alone, without substantial microbial preconditioning, contributes much to the probability that a leaf will enter a depositional environment in a recognizable form. The results of experiments with whole fresh leaves show that they are more resistant to fragmentation than leaves exposed to microbiological attack. Unless the leaf is exceptionally large or small, leaf size and thickness are not likely to be as critical in determining the preservation potential of a leaf type as the rate of microbiological degradation.

PLAY

1. The passage is primarily concerned with

   (A) Why leaves disintegrate

   (B) An analysis of leaf structure and composition

   (C) Comparing lakes and streams

   (D) The purpose of particle feeders

   (E) How leaves' mechanical strength is affected by microbiological activity

The passage reads primarily about leaves, making that its primary concern, so eliminate Choices (C) and (D) right off. Choice (A) is too broad, as other causes of disintegration may exist that the passage doesn't mention. Choice (B) is too specific: The passage mentions leaf structure, but not as its primary focus. Correct answer: Choice (E).

2. Which of the following is mentioned as a reason for leaf degradation in streams? Consider each of the three choices separately and select all that apply.

   (A) Mechanical damage

   (B) Biological degradation

   (C) Large particle feeders

The second paragraph of the passage tells you that "loss of material in stream-processed leaves is a combination of biological and mechanical degradation." Choice (C) is incorrect because the passage specifically states that the pattern of holes is contrary to that of large particle feeders. The correct answers are Choices (A) and (B).

3. The conclusion that the author reached from Ferguson's revolving drum experiment was that

(A) Leaf thickness is only a contributing factor to leaf fragmentation.

(B) Leaves submerged in water degrade more rapidly than leaves deposited in mud or silt.

(C) Leaves with a strong midrib deteriorate less than leaves without such a midrib.

(D) Microbial attack is made worse by high temperatures.

(E) Bimodal distribution reduces leaf attrition.

The middle of the last paragraph tells you that leaf thickness *alone* is unlikely to affect the final form of the leaf. You probably need to reread that sentence a few times to get past the jargon, but a detail or fact question is the type of question you should be sure to answer correctly. Choice (B) introduces facts not discussed in the passage; the passage doesn't talk of leaves in mud or silt. Choice (C) is mentioned in the passage but not in Ferguson's experiments.

Nothing about high temperatures appears in the passage, which eliminates Choice (D). Choice (E) sounds pretentious and pompous — and nice and scientific — but has nothing to do with Ferguson. To answer this question correctly, you need to return to the passage to look up Ferguson specifically, not merely rely on your memory of the passage as a whole. Correct answer: Choice (A).

Be careful to answer *only* what the question is asking. Answer-choice traps include statements that are true but don't answer the question.

WARNING **4.** The tone of the passage is

(A) Persuasive

(B) Biased

(C) Objective

(D) Argumentative

(E) Disparaging

The passage is hardly persuasive; it isn't really trying to change your opinion on an issue. It objectively presents scientific facts and experimental evidence. Because you know the gist of the passage and the context of each paragraph, the answer is obvious. Correct answer: Choice (C).

5. Select the sentence in the fourth paragraph that explains the form of mechanical breakdown of most species of leaves.

Skim for key words to answer this question. The first and only place *mechanical breakdown* is mentioned is in the first sentence of the fourth paragraph. Correct answer: "In most species, the mechanical breakdown will take the form of gradual attrition at the margins."

6. Which would be an example of "energy of the environment" (fourth paragraph, second sentence)?

(A) Wind and rain

(B) Sunlight

(C) Animals that eat leaves

(D) Lumberjacks

(E) Fuel that may be harvested

The passage is about the degradation of leaves, which you already know. The fourth paragraph discusses factors that may break a brittle leaf across its center, or midrib. Sunlight may do this, but it wouldn't necessarily target the midrib, so out with Choice (B). Animals would digest the leaves such that the leaves wouldn't degrade, so no more Choice (C). Lumberjacks may leave leaves behind (so to speak), but the passage is all about natural factors, so down with Choice (D). Finally, there's nothing about harvesting fuel, so Choice (E) is out. This leaves Choice (A), wind and rain, which makes sense. The wind and rain physically affect the leaf and both cause degradation and breaking along its weak point, the midrib. Correct answer: Choice (A).

THE SOCIAL SCIENCES PASSAGE

The GRE usually includes a social sciences passage about history, psychology, business, or a variety of other topics. If the social sciences passage offers a perspective on a subject that you may already be familiar with, you can use your understanding of the subject as a backdrop to make the passage easier to read and understand.

TIP Within each section, you can work the passages in any order. If you find that you prefer a social sciences passage over a biological or physical science passage, you can work the passage you prefer first.

Here's a social sciences passage. Though you need to read the passage more carefully, the underlying strategy is the same: Look for the gist of the passage, usually in the first paragraph, and identify the purpose of each paragraph thereafter. You'll still need to revisit these paragraphs to find details, so knowing where the details are located is easier and more useful than memorizing them.

Multinational corporations frequently encounter impediments in their attempts to explain to politicians, human rights groups, and (perhaps most importantly) their consumer base why they do business with, and even seek closer business ties to, countries whose human rights records are considered heinous by United States standards. The CEOs propound that in the business trenches, the issue of human rights must effectively be detached from the wider spectrum of free trade. Discussion of the uneasy alliance between trade and human rights has trickled down from the boardrooms of large multinational corporations to the consumer on the street who, given the wide variety of products available to him, is eager to show support for human rights by boycotting the products of a company he feels does not do enough to help its overseas workers. International human rights organizations also are pressuring the multinationals to push for more humane working conditions in other countries and to, in effect, develop a code of business conduct that must be adhered to if the American company is to continue working with the overseas partner.

The president, in drawing up a plan for what he calls the "economic architecture of our times," wants economists, business leaders, and human rights groups to work together to develop a set of principles that the foreign partners of United States corporations will voluntarily embrace. Human rights activists, incensed at the nebulous plans for implementing such rules, charge that their agenda is being given low priority by the State Department. The president vociferously denies their charges, arguing that each situation is approached on its merits without prejudice, and hopes that all the groups can work together to develop principles based on empirical research rather than political fiat, emphasizing that the businesses with experience in the field must initiate the process of developing such guidelines. Business leaders, while paying lip service to the concept of these principles, fight stealthily against their formal endorsement because they fear such "voluntary" concepts may someday be given the force of law. Few business leaders have forgotten the Sullivan Principles, in which a set of voluntary rules regarding business conduct with South Africa (giving benefits to workers and banning apartheid in the companies that worked with U.S. partners) became legislation.

PLAY

7. Which of the following best states the central idea of the passage?

(A) Politicians are quixotic in their assessment of the priorities of the State Department.

(B) Multinational corporations have little if any influence on the domestic policies of their overseas partners.

(C) Voluntary principles that are turned into law are unconstitutional.

(D) Disagreement exists between the desires of human rights activists to improve the working conditions of overseas workers and the pragmatic approach taken by the corporations.

(E) It is inappropriate to expect foreign corporations to adhere to American standards.

In Choice (A), the word *quixotic* means idealistic or impractical. The word comes from the fictional character Don Quixote, who tilted at windmills. (*Tilting* refers to a knight on horseback tilting his joust toward a target for the purpose of attack.) Although the president in this passage may not be realistic in his assessment of State Department policies, his belief isn't the main idea of the passage.

Choice (E) is a value judgment. An answer that passes judgment, saying something is right or wrong, better or worse, or more or less appropriate (as in this case), is almost never the correct answer.

The main idea of any passage is usually stated in the first sentence or two. The first sentence of this passage touches on the difficulties that corporations have in explaining their business ties with certain countries to politicians, human rights groups, and consumers. From this statement, you may infer that those groups disagree with the policies of the corporations. Correct answer: Choice (D).

TIP

Just because a statement is true doesn't necessarily mean it's the correct answer to the question, especially a main idea question. All the answer choices are typically true statements, though only one is the main idea.

8. According to the passage, the president wants the voluntary principles to be initiated by businesses rather than by politicians or human rights activists because

(A) Businesses have empirical experience in the field and thus know what the conditions are and how they may/should be remedied.

(B) Businesses make profits from the labor of the workers and thus have a moral obligation to improve their employees' working conditions.

(C) Workers will not accept principles drawn up by politicians whom they distrust but may agree to principles created by the corporations that pay them.

(D) Foreign nations are distrustful of U.S. political intervention and are more likely to accept suggestions from multinational corporations.

(E) Political activist groups have concerns that are too dramatically different from those of the corporations for the groups to be able to work together.

TIP

When a question begins with the words *according to the passage*, you need to go back to the passage and find the answer. *Empirical* is the key word here, buried in the middle of the second paragraph.

Find the word and read the sentence, and you've found the answer: "The president vociferously denies their charges, arguing that each situation is approached on its merits without prejudice, and hopes that all the groups can work together to develop principles based on *empirical research* rather than political fiat, emphasizing that the *businesses with experience in the field must initiate the process* of developing such guidelines." You don't even need to know what *empirical* (derived from observation or experiment) means. The reasoning of Choices (B), (C), (D), and (E) isn't stated in the passage. Correct answer: Choice (A).

9. Select the sentence from the second paragraph that describes the human rights activists' response to the president's plan.

The passage contains only one mention of *human rights activists*, and it appears in the second sentence of the second paragraph. So the correct answer is "Human rights activists, incensed at the nebulous plans for implementing such rules, charge that their agenda is being given low priority by the State Department."

10. Which of the following is a reason the author mentions the boycott of a corporation's products by its customers? Consider each of the three choices separately and select all that apply.

   (A) To show the difficulties that arise when corporations attempt to become involved in politics

   (B) To suggest the possibility of failure of any plan that does not account for the customer's perspective

   (C) To indicate the pressures that are on the multinational corporations

Choice (A) makes a valid point. Difficulties may arise when corporations attempt to become involved in politics. However, the passage doesn't give that as a reason for a boycott, so Choice (A) is wrong. Choice (B) seems logical because a company that ignores its customers will probably fail. The passage mentions corporate communications with customers in the first sentence but not the customer's perspective, so Choice (B) is wrong. Choice (C) is also true, because according to the passage, multinational corporations run the risk of alienating any group and thus inciting a boycott, which is a reason given by the passage. Correct answer: Choice (C).

REMEMBER

Just because you *can* choose more than one answer doesn't mean you *have* to. (Except on Sentence Equivalence, where the instructions specifically indicate *two* answers.) These questions can have one, two, or three correct answers. Never zero, though.

11. Which of the following statements about the Sullivan Principles can best be inferred from the passage?

   (A) They had a detrimental effect on the profits of those corporations doing business with South Africa.

   (B) They represented an improper alliance between political and business groups.

   (C) They placed the needs of the foreign workers over those of the domestic workers whose jobs would therefore be in jeopardy.

   (D) They will be used as a model to create future voluntary business guidelines.

   (E) They will have a chilling effect on future adoption of voluntary guidelines.

Choice (A) is the trap here. Perhaps you assumed that because the companies seem to dislike the Sullivan Principles, they hurt company profits. However, the passage says nothing about profits. Maybe the companies still made good profits but objected to the Sullivan Principles, well, on principle. The companies just may not have wanted governmental intervention, even if profits weren't decreased.

The key words to search for are *Sullivan Principles;* then read around them. The Principles appear in the last sentence, and just before that, the passage states that business leaders "*fear* such 'voluntary' concepts may someday be given the force of law." Because business leaders fear that the adoption of voluntary guidelines will lead to forced legislation, the Sullivan Principles will have a chilling effect on the future adoption of voluntary guidelines. The correct answer is Choice (E).

THE HUMANITIES PASSAGE

A humanities passage may be about art, music, philosophy, drama, or literature. It typically places its subject in a positive light, especially if it's about a person who was a pioneer in his or her field, such as the first African American astronaut or the first female doctor. Use this to your advantage: If someone is worthy of mention historically or in a Reading Comprehension passage, then he or she probably was an amazing person or did something truly noteworthy. Look for this sense of admiration from the author to create the context in which to frame the passage.

REMEMBER

The humanities passages seem to be the most down-to-earth of the lot. They're easy to read, informative, and can even be enjoyable. Too bad they're rare. The approach is the same, though: Look for the gist of the passage in a few words and establish a context for the whole story and each paragraph. You can always go back for the details later.

REMEMBER

Although the passage doesn't require meticulous reading, the questions are another matter. The questions following a humanities passage often require you to get into the mind of the author in order to read between the lines and make inferences. While you're reading a passage about a particular person, for example, try to ascertain not just what the person accomplished but why this person worked toward those goals and what mark was left on the world.

Here's an example of a typical humanities passage, taken from *LSAT For Dummies* by Amy Hackney Blackwell (Wiley), about someone you've probably never heard of before but will still enjoy reading about.

Junzaburou Nishiwaki, a 20th-century Japanese poet, scholar, and translator, spent his career working to introduce Japanese readers to European and American writing and to break his country out of its literary insularity. He was interested in European culture all his life. Born to a wealthy family in rural Niigata prefecture in 1894, Nishiwaki spent his youth aspiring to be a painter and traveled to Tokyo in 1911 to study fused Japanese and European artistic traditions. After his father died in 1913, Nishiwaki studied economics at Keio University, but his real love was English literature. After graduating, he worked for several years as a reporter at the English-language *Japan Times* and as a teacher at Keio University.

Nishiwaki finally received the opportunity to concentrate on English literature in 1922, when Keio University sent him to Oxford University for three years. He spent this time reading literature in Old and Middle English and classical Greek and Latin. He became fluent in English, French, German, Latin, and Greek. While he was in England, Roaring Twenties modernism caught his eye, and the works of writers such as James Joyce, Ezra Pound, and T. S. Eliot were crucially important to his literary development. In 1925, Nishiwaki published his first book, *Spectrum,* a volume of poems written in English. He explained that English offered him much more freedom of expression than traditional Japanese poetic language.

Nishiwaki returned to Keio University in 1925 and became a professor of English literature, teaching linguistics, Old and Middle English, and the history of English literature. He remained active in modernist and avant-garde literary circles. In 1933 he published *Ambarvalia,* his first volume of poetry written in Japanese; this collection of surrealist verse ranged far and wide through European geography and history and included Japanese translations of Catullus, Sophocles, and Shakespeare. Angered by the Japanese government's fascist policies, Nishiwaki refused to write poetry during the Second World War. He spent the war years writing a dissertation on ancient Germanic literature.

After the war, Nishiwaki resumed his poetic pursuits and in 1947 published *Tabibito kaerazu,* in which he abandoned modernist language and returned to a classical Japanese poetic style but with his own postmodernist touch, incorporating both Eastern and Western literary traditions. In 1953, Nishiwaki published *Kindai no guuwa,* which critics consider his most poetically mature work. He spent his last years producing works of such writers as D. H. Lawrence, James Joyce, T. S. Eliot, Stéphane Mallarmé, Shakespeare, and Chaucer. Nishiwaki retired from Keio University in 1962, though he continued to teach and write poetry. Before his death in 1982, he received numerous honors and awards; he was appointed to the Japanese Academy of Arts and Sciences, named a Person of Cultural Merit, and nominated for the Nobel Prize by Ezra Pound. Critics today consider Nishiwaki to have exercised more influence on younger poets than any other Japanese poet since 1945.

12. Which one of the following most accurately states the main idea of the passage?

(A) Nishiwaki was a Japanese poet who rebelled against the strictures of his country's government and protested its policies toward Europe during World War II.

(B) Nishiwaki was a Japanese poet and literary critic who embraced European literature as a way of rebelling against the constraints of his family and traditional Japanese culture.

(C) Nishiwaki was a Japanese poet and professor who spent his life trying to convince young Japanese students that European literary forms were superior to Japanese poetic styles.

(D) Nishiwaki was a Japanese poet and linguist who throughout his life chose to write in English rather than Japanese.

(E) Nishiwaki was a Japanese poet and scholar who spent his life specializing in European literature, which proved tremendously influential to his own work.

A process of elimination reveals the correct answer. Choice (A) is wrong: Though Nishiwaki did protest against his country's fascist policies during World War II, this fact isn't the main idea of the passage. Choice (B) is flat-out wrong: Although the first paragraph discusses Nishiwaki's departure from family and his country's literary insularity, the word *rebelling* is too harsh. Choice (C) is also wrong: The passage doesn't say that he tried to convince his students one way or the other. Choice (D) is wrong: The passage states only that his first book was in English and many others were in Japanese. Correct answer: Choice (E).

13. The author's attitude toward Nishiwaki's life and career can be best described as

(A) Scholarly interest in the life and works of a significant literary figure

(B) Mild surprise at Nishiwaki's choosing to write poetry in a language foreign to him

(C) Open admiration for Nishiwaki's ability to function in several languages

(D) Skepticism toward Nishiwaki's motives in refusing to write poetry during the Second World War

(E) Envy of Nishiwaki's success in publishing and academia

Choices (B), (D), and (E) are wrong because the passage doesn't reflect surprise, skepticism, or envy. Choices (A) and (C) remain, but you can eliminate Choice (C): The passage is objective, not admiring, and Nishiwaki's multilingual ability is a supporting detail to his accomplishments. The correct answer is Choice (A).

14. The primary function of the first paragraph is to

(A) Describe Nishiwaki's brief study of painting

(B) Introduce Nishiwaki and his lifelong interest in European culture

(C) Summarize Nishiwaki's contribution to Japanese literature

(D) Explain why a Japanese man chose to specialize in English literature

(E) Analyze European contributions to Japanese culture at the start of the 20th century

After rereading the first paragraph, you know that in a nutshell it introduces Nishiwaki as one who worked to bridge the literature gap separating Japan from Europe and America. It also summarizes Nishiwaki's interest in art through college and his early career years afterward. Most importantly, the first paragraph sets the stage for the rest of the essay. Armed with this perspective, only one possible answer remains: Choice (B).

15. Select the sentence in the third paragraph that explains why Nishiwaki stopped writing poetry during World War II.

Like most select-a-sentence questions, look for the correct sentence buried in the passage. Correct answer: "Angered by the Japanese government's fascist policies, Nishiwaki refused to write poetry during the Second World War."

16. The passage is primarily concerned with

(A) Comparing Nishiwaki's poetry to that of other Japanese poets of the 20th century

(B) Discussing the role of the avant-garde movement in Nishiwaki's writing

(C) Providing a brief biography of Nishiwaki that explains the significance of his work

(D) Explaining why writers can benefit from studying literature from other countries

(E) Describing the transformation in Japanese poetic style during the post-war period

The key words in this question are *primarily concerned with.* The passage may suggest some of the points listed, but its *primary concern* is more explicit. Choice (A) is wrong because the author doesn't mention the work of other Japanese poets. Choice (B) is wrong because although the avant-garde movement was influential to Nishiwaki's writing, this point is hardly the primary concern. Choice (C) looks about right, but check the others just in case. Choice (D) is wrong because the author doesn't mention the benefits of studying foreign literature. Choice (E) is wrong because the passage doesn't mention changes in Japanese poetic style after the war. Correct answer: Choice (C).

17. According to the passage, which one of the following types of literature did *not* greatly interest Nishiwaki? Consider each of the three choices separately and select all that apply.

(A) Old and Middle English literature such as *Beowulf* and *The Canterbury Tales*

(B) Classical Greek works such as *Antigone*

(C) Classical Japanese literature such as *The Tale of Genji*

From the first paragraph, you know that Nishiwaki's real love was English literature. From the second paragraph, you know that Nishiwaki spent his time at Oxford reading Old and Middle English and classical Greek and Latin. However, even though he may have had some interest in Japanese literature, it didn't *greatly* interest him as the question states. Only one correct answer: Choice (C).

18. Select the sentence in the second paragraph that explains why Nishiwaki chose to write his first published poems in English.

Though many sentences in the passage mention Nishiwaki's interest in English literature, in only one sentence does the passage provide Nishiwaki's explanation of why he chose to write his first published poems in English. Correct answer: "He explained that English offered him much more freedom of expression than traditional Japanese poetic language."

THE SOCIAL SCIENCES PASSAGE REDUX

The previous three passages are good segues to the way the GRE thinks and phrases its questions. However, not all the passages are as *accessible* (easy) as these. Practice your chops on this challenging social sciences passage.

This passage is an excerpt from *The Wiley-Blackwell Companion to Sociology*, edited by George Ritzer (Wiley-Blackwell).

PLAY

Ritzer (2009) has recently argued that the focus on either production or consumption has always been misplaced and that all acts always involve both. That is, all acts of production and consumption are fundamentally acts of prosumption. The assembly-line worker is always consuming all sorts of things (parts, energy, tools) in the process of production, and conversely the consumer in, for example, a fast food restaurant is always producing (garnishes for a sandwich, soft drinks from the self-serve dispenser, the disposal of debris derived from the meal). This suggests a dramatic reorientation of theorizing about the economy away from production or consumption and in the direction of prosumption.

Prosumption is not only a historical reality, but it is becoming increasingly ubiquitous with the emergence on the internet of Web 2.0. Web 1.0 (e.g., AOL) typically involved sites that were created and managed by producers and used more or less passively by separable consumers. The latter not only did not produce the websites, but usually could not alter their content in any meaningful way. In contrast, Web 2.0 is defined by sites (e.g., Facebook, blogs) the contents of which are produced, wholly (blogs) or in part (Facebook), by the user. While everything about some 2.0 sites (a blog, for example) is likely produced by those who also consume them, on others (the Facebook page) the basic structure of the site is created by the producer, while all of the content comes from the consumer(s). Even though something of the distinction between producer and consumer remains in the latter case, it is clear that Web 2.0 is the paradigmatic domain of the prosumer. As the internet continues to evolve, we can expect to see more and more user-generated content and therefore an even greater role for the prosumer.

Of course, this shift to prosumption does not mean that sociological theorists should ignore production (the production end of the prosumption continuum) or consumption (the consumption end of that continuum). On the production side, there is certainly no end of issues to concern the theorist. Among others, there is David Harvey's (2005) interest in, and critique of, neoliberalism, as well as Hardt and Negri's (2000) interest in the transformation of the capitalist and proletariat into Empire and Multitude in the global age.

19. What does Ritzer argue is the difference between production and consumption?

(A) Production is creating, and consuming is using.

(B) Production is recent, and consumption is historical.

(C) Production is permanent, and consumption is temporary.

(D) They are opposite sides of the same spectrum.

(E) They are not different.

In the first paragraph, Ritzer declares that "all acts always involve both" and that "all acts of production and consumption are fundamentally part of prosumption." Therefore, to Ritzer, they're part of the same spectrum. The correct choice is (D).

20. According to the passage, Unlike Web 1.0, Web 2.0 is specifically

(A) Newer and therefore better

(B) Fueled by content produced by the user

(C) An asset to the neo-liberal market forces

(D) A reflection of the distinction between the producer and the consumer

(E) Designed for heavy reliance by the consumer

The second paragraph states that "Web 2.0 is defined by sites (e.g., Facebook, blogs) the contents of which are produced, wholly (blogs) or in part (Facebook), by the user," making the correct answer Choice (B).

21. According to the passage, the emergence of Web 2.0 is an example of

   (A) Production

   (B) Consumption

   (C) Prosumption

   (D) Neo-liberalism

   (E) Social networking

The second paragraph of Passage 1 states that "prosumption [. . .] is becoming increasingly ubiquitous with the emergence [. . .] of Web 2.0." The correct answer is Choice (C).

22. What is the primary purpose of the passage?

   (A) To explain the success of Web 2.0 sites such as Facebook

   (B) To describe the shift to prosumption and the accompanying emergence of Web 2.0

   (C) To portray the perspective of sociological theorists, such as Harvey, on neoliberalism

   (D) To depict the observation of sociological theorists, such as Hardt and Negri, on the transformation of the capitalist and proletariat into Empire and Multitude

   (E) To describe the inevitable path of the prosumer

The passage opens with the description of prosumption, then exemplifies it with Web 2.0, and then closes with the effects of prosumption. Though the passage mentions the topics of the other answer choices, none of these is the primary purpose of the passage, and the correct answer is Choice (B).

Argument analysis

PLAY

A recent study of the Alhambra High School District shows a two-point increase in truancy in its high schools from the previous year to 14.5 percent. Participation in after-school programs has decreased by 22 percent. The Alhambra High School District is obviously failing in its mission to improve academic success.

The argument that the Alhambra High School District is failing to improve academic success is based on which of the following assumptions?

Set up the *because* and *therefore* premise:

» **Because** truancy increased and after-school participation declined,

» **Therefore** the high school is failing in its mission to improve academic success.

The argument assumes that academic success is tied to truancy and after-school participation.

   (A) The Alhambra High School District doesn't have sufficient funding to enforce attendance or improve after-school programs.

   (B) Attendance has remained unchanged at the elementary and middle-school levels.

   (C) Private schools and charter schools have had significantly improved academic success.

   (D) Attendance and after-school participation are accurate measures of academic success.

   (E) The Alhambra High School District has increased focus to improving its athletic program.

Now eliminate each choice, one by one:

>> Choice (A) is wrong, because funding is outside the scope of the argument.

>> Choice (B) is wrong, because elementary and middle schools are also outside the scope of the argument.

>> Choice (C) is wrong, because private and charter schools are outside the scope of the argument.

>> Choice (D) is correct, because the argument uses reduced attendance and after-school participation as its evidence that academic success is failing.

>> Choice (E) is wrong because the athletic program is out of scope of the argument.

The correct answer is Choice (D).

PLAY

For healthcare and health insurance to become less expensive, the federal government first needs to implement cost-control measures in the healthcare industry. Tort reform is the obvious place to start. The costs of medical malpractice insurance and lawsuits are skyrocketing, and medical professionals simply increase the cost of their services to keep pace. Tort reform would significantly reduce the number of frivolous malpractice claims, limit the damage awarded to plaintiffs, and reduce the cost of malpractice insurance. Healthcare providers and insurance companies could then pass the savings along to consumers. Until some sort of tort reform effectively addresses this issue, healthcare will continue to be expensive regardless of whether people are paying out of pocket or through a government-administered program.

Which of the following statements most accurately identifies the assumption that must be true for the argument to be true?

Set up the *because* and *therefore* premise:

>> **Because** malpractice insurance and lawsuits are expensive,

>> **Therefore** reducing these costs will bring down the price of healthcare.

The argument assumes that malpractice insurance and lawsuits are the key drivers of inflated healthcare costs.

(A) Medical insurance will increase the cost of healthcare services.

(B) Medical insurance costs are rising.

(C) The costs of malpractice insurance and lawsuits drive up the healthcare costs.

(D) Providers are responsible for the high healthcare costs.

(E) Tort reform would reduce medical malpractice litigation and limit damages awarded to plaintiffs.

Now eliminate each choice, one by one:

>> Choice (A) is wrong, because it merely repeats information stated in the passage.

>> Choice (B) is wrong, because it simply restates the problem.

>> Choice (C) is correct, because it restates the assumption: that insurance and lawsuits drive up the cost of healthcare.

>> Choice (D) is wrong, because it's too vague — it doesn't describe how providers drive up the costs.

>> Choice (E) is wrong because it restates the argument, but it doesn't say *how* tort reform would help.

The correct answer is Choice (C).

PLAY

In earlier versions of the GRE, approximately 6 percent of test-takers achieved perfect quantitative scores, while almost no test-takers answered more than 60 percent of the verbal questions correctly. Because approximately one in 17 test-takers scored perfect quantitative scores of 800 (based on the old scoring scale), **a perfect or near-perfect GRE quantitative score did not help distinguish a truly competitive applicant.** The current version of the GRE, released in 2011, resolves this discrepancy by **featuring more challenging questions in the quantitative sections** and simplifying the verbal sections.

In the argument given, the two **bolded phrases** play which of the following roles?

Set up the *because* and *therefore* premise:

>> **Because** on the old GRE, too many test-takers achieved perfect quantitative scores,

>> **Therefore** the current GRE features a more challenging quantitative section.

TIP

This is a different and less common format of the Analyzing an Argument question, but the premise is exactly the same. As long as you establish the *Because/Therefore* relationship and answer the question yourself, the wrong answers are easy to eliminate.

(A) The first describes a hypothesis which the second opposes; the second is an alternative explanation.

(B) The first describes the result of a problem; the second describes a solution to that problem.

(C) The first proposes a solution to a problem described by the second; the second is that problem.

(D) The first is a claim of the result of a problem described by the second; the second is a problem with the claim described by the first.

(E) The first describes a requirement of the argument to revise its initial formulation of the position it seeks to establish; the second presents that position in a revised form.

Now eliminate each choice, one by one:

>> Choice (A) is wrong, because the second phrase doesn't oppose the first one.

TIP

Choice (A) is a standard wrong answer. Typically, a few of the answer choices will suggest that the two phrases "oppose" or "counter" each other. This may be true, but you can quickly scan the passage to make sure the phrases agree, and if they do, you can eliminate any answer choices that suggest they contradict.

>> Choice (B) is correct, because the first phrase describes the problem with the easy quantitative section, and the second phrase describes the solution that ETS put into place.

>> Choice (C) is wrong, because it gets the phrases backwards — the first phrase describes a problem, and the second phrase proposes a solution.

>> Choice (D) is wrong, because it hardly makes sense — a true tactic of this question format, suggesting it's a trap answer designed to take up your time.

>> Choice (E) is wrong for the same reason as Choice (D) — it's a wordy, nonsense trap designed to absorb your time.

TIP

Choices (D) and (E) illustrate why it's imperative to *answer the question yourself first* — so that when you see a nonsensical, wordy answer, you don't spend a whole lot of time checking whether it's true.

The correct answer is Choice (B).

Block 3
Tallying Up the Math You Need to Know

This block is a rundown of all the math you thought you'd never need again, but actually do need to know to do well on the GRE. Start with basic math, including operations, units of measurement, decimals, fractions, percentages, and ratios. Next, brush up on solving for x, working with roots and radicals, and graphing x and y on the coordinate plane. You also find core GRE geometry concepts and tips for untangling story-based word problems about number of possible outcomes or the probability of something happening. Last but not least, you'll review basic statistics, drawing conclusions from tables and graphs, and unravel the strategies you need for Quantitative Comparison questions. Throughout this block, you encounter example questions and explanations that help you test your renewed math skills.

Working with Numbers and Operations

If you've forgotten even the basics, this section is for you. Uncover terms and concepts you likely recognize but need to practice before the GRE, like absolute value, multiplying and dividing fractions, and ratios.

Math terms

GRE math questions may use some math terminology when referring to values. A question might read "x is an integer" or "x is a factor of 21." You're expected to know what these terms mean: Integer, whole number, real number, non-real number, factor, multiple, and prime number.

The GRE may describe the steps you take with the math. Instead of a nice, simple "$5 - 4 =$," the GRE asks something like "What is the difference of five and four?" That's fine as long as you know what it's asking. Just to be sure, here are some common math terms: sum, product, difference, and quotient.

If you need to review any of these terms, check out Khan Academy (www.khanacademy.org) or your favorite math resource online.

Prime and composite numbers

Any whole number greater than 1 is either prime or composite. A *prime number* is a whole number that has exactly two positive factors: 1 and itself. Examples of prime numbers include 2, 3, 5, 7, and 11.

TIP

The GRE expects you to know these key specifics when dealing with prime numbers:

>> Zero isn't prime because it's not positive and can't be factored.

>> One isn't prime because it has only *one* factor: itself. (A prime number has *two* factors.)

>> Two is the *only even* prime number because it's the only even number with exactly two factors: 1 and itself.

Meanwhile, a *composite number* has more than two factors, meaning that it can be divided into smaller integers and primes. Examples of composite numbers include 4, 6, 8, and 9.

REMEMBER

Any composite number factors to prime numbers. 12 factors to $2 \times 2 \times 3$; 84 factors to $2 \times 2 \times 3 \times 7$; and 125 factors to $5 \times 5 \times 5$. This process is called *prime factorization*.

Here's an example GRE question that challenges your grasp of prime numbers:

PLAY

Quantity A	*Quantity B*
The number of prime numbers from 0 to 10, inclusive	The number of prime numbers from 11 to 20, inclusive

(A) Quantity A is greater.

(B) Quantity B is greater.

(C) The two quantities are equal.

(D) The relationship cannot be determined from the information given.

In Quantity A, the prime numbers from 0 to 10, inclusive, are 2, 3, 5, and 7. In Quantity B, the prime numbers from 11 to 20, inclusive, are 11, 13, 17, and 19. Both quantities have four prime numbers, but counting 0 or 1 as prime (which you know not to do) would lead you to choose (A), which is incorrect. The correct answer is (C).

The units digit

The *units digit* is the single number before the decimal or the ending number of any integer. In the number 654.37, for example, the units digit is 4, and in 298, the units digit is 8. When you multiply two integers, the units digit of the product comes from the units digit of the numbers multiplied.

Any integer ending in a 4 times any integer ending in a 3 results in an integer ending in a 2, because $4 \times 3 = 12$, and 12 ends in a 2. Check out these examples:

$$14 \times 13 = 182$$
$$24 \times 43 = 1,032$$
$$204 \times 103 = 21,012$$

Whatever integers you multiply, if one ends in a 4 and the other ends in a 3, the product ends in a 2. But this is true with all integers, not just 4 and 3. Integers ending in 6 and 3, for example, result in a product ending in 8, because $6 \times 3 = 18$:

Who knew? Anyway, this comes up in the GRE, so try this example.

$$n = (99)^2$$

Quantity A	_Quantity B_
The units digit of n	1

(A) Quantity A is greater.

(B) Quantity B is greater.

(C) The two quantities are equal.

(D) The relationship cannot be determined from the information given.

You could multiply the 99s, but you don't have to. Instead, just multiply the units digits: $9 \times 9 = 81$, so the units digit of n is 1 and the answer is (C).

Absolute value

The *absolute value*, indicated by two vertical parallel lines, is the positive form of a number. Technically, *absolute value* refers to the expression's distance from 0 on the number line. Because -7 is 7 units from 0, the absolute value of -7, written as $|-7|$, is 7.

The GRE likes to play with absolute values and catch you with double negatives. $-|-3|$ is the same thing as $-(+3)$, which equals -3. The trick is taking the calculations step by step. The absolute value of -3 is 3, which you make negative to get -3.

Try this one:

$-|-|-5|| =$

Take this example step by step, from the inside out. Say to yourself, "The absolute value of -5 is 5. Then the negative of that is -5. Then the absolute value of that is 5. And finally, the negative of that is -5."

This example is like a sentence that reads, "The committee voted against stopping the proposition from not happening." Wait — was the committee *for* or *against* the proposition? Break the sentence (or equation) down piece by piece to resolve the double negatives.

If you have an x or another unknown inside the absolute-value expression, it means that the expression is that distance from 0 on the number line and typically could be in two separate places. For example, $|x| = 7$ tells you that x is 7 away from 0 on the number line, but you don't know whether it's on the positive or negative side, so x could equal 7 or -7. Couple of things just to be clear:

>> **Any x has _one_ value.** You don't know which one it is without more information. (With $|x| = 7$, something like $x > 0$ would do the trick.)

>> **Any absolute value is always _positive_.** A number can't be a negative distance from 0, so an equation like $|x| = -5$ is impossible or, in math, has *no solution*.

Order of operations

When you encounter a question on the GRE that includes several operations (addition, subtraction, multiplication, division, squaring, and so on), you must perform those operations in the following order to arrive at the correct answer:

1. Parentheses

Start with what's inside the parentheses. If they're nested (meaning parentheses inside other parentheses), work the inside parentheses first.

2. Exponents

Any exponents are next.

3. Multiplication or division

Work multiplication and division next.

4. Addition or subtraction

Finally, add or subtract.

REMEMBER

Use the mnemonic *Please Excuse My Dear Aunt Sally (PEMDAS)*, which of course is *Parentheses, Exponents, Multiplication, Division, Addition, and Subtraction.*

PLAY

Use PEMDAS for this problem:

$$10(3-5)^2$$

Start with what's inside the parentheses: $3-5 = -2$. Then move on to the exponents: -2 squared equals 4. Finally, do the multiplication: $4 \times 10 = 40$. The correct answer is 40.

Fractions

You probably got fractions just fine back in middle school. This section helps you refresh what you learned.

Adding and subtracting

REMEMBER

You can add and subtract fractions with a *common denominator* (the same bottom part of the fraction). If the fractions don't have a common denominator, give them one; then add or subtract them with the *numerator* (the top part of the fraction).

PLAY

$$\frac{2}{5} + \frac{3}{7} =$$

Here, 5 and 7 are different denominators, so you can't add these two fractions. Make the denominators the same, however, and then you *can* add the fractions.

To change the denominator without changing the fraction's value, multiply the fraction's top and bottom by the same number. You're not changing the fraction's value because you're essentially multiplying each fraction by 1:

$$\frac{7}{7} = 1 \quad \text{and} \quad \frac{5}{5} = 1$$

Use this method to give the fractions common denominators:

$$\frac{2}{5} \times \frac{7}{7} = \frac{14}{35} \quad \text{and} \quad \frac{3}{7} \times \frac{5}{5} = \frac{15}{35}$$

Now that the denominators are the same, add the fractions:

$$\frac{14}{35} + \frac{15}{35} = \frac{29}{35}$$

Multiplying

To multiply fractions, just go straight across, multiplying the numerators together and the denominators together:

$$\frac{2}{5} \times \frac{3}{7} = \frac{2 \times 3}{5 \times 7} = \frac{6}{35}$$

Always check whether you can cancel out common factors between a numerator and a denominator before you begin multiplying. This approach simplifies the work and makes it easier to reduce fractions at the end. Typical GRE math questions are set up to do this.

To multiply these fractions:

$$\frac{6}{5} \times \frac{4}{9}$$

You could just multiply straight across, which will work, but note that the 6 and the 9 are each divisible by 3. It's easier to cancel those 3s from the numerator and denominator and *then* multiply:

$$\frac{^2\cancel{6}}{5} \times \frac{4}{\cancel{9}_3} = \frac{2}{5} \times \frac{4}{3} = \frac{8}{15}$$

Or with this example:

$$\frac{4}{15} \times \frac{5}{8}$$

Before you multiply these, reduce the 4 and the 8 (each is divisible by 4), along with the 15 and the 5 (both by 5), simplifying the problem:

$$\frac{^1\cancel{4}}{\cancel{15}_3} \times \frac{^1\cancel{5}}{\cancel{8}_2} = \frac{1}{3} \times \frac{1}{2} = \frac{1}{6}$$

Dividing

To divide two fractions, you *reciprocate* the second fraction (flip it over) and then multiply them:

$$\frac{1}{3} \div \frac{2}{5} = \frac{1}{3} \times \frac{5}{2} = \frac{5}{6}$$

Mixed numbers and improper fractions

A *mixed number* is a whole number with a fraction, such as $2\frac{1}{3}$ or $4\frac{2}{5}$. Before you can add, subtract, multiply, or divide a mixed number, you have to get it into fraction form. To do this, multiply the denominator (bottom number) by the whole number and add that to the numerator (top number); then put the sum over the denominator:

$$\gg \ 2\frac{1}{3}=\frac{(3\times2)+1}{3}=\frac{7}{3}$$

$$\gg \ 4\frac{2}{5}=\frac{(5\times4)+2}{5}=\frac{22}{5}$$

The result is an *improper fraction,* in which the numerator is larger than the denominator. Converting an improper fraction back to a mixed number is less common, but to do so, divide the numerator by the denominator, write down the whole number, and then place the remainder over the denominator.

To convert the improper fraction $\frac{22}{7}$ to a mixed number, divide the 7 into 22, and you get 3 with a remainder of 1. The 7 stays as the denominator, and the resulting mixed number is $3\frac{1}{7}$.

Cross-multiplying

To cross-multiply, multiply the top of one fraction by the bottom of the other fraction, and set the quantities equal to each other:

$$\frac{4}{5}=\frac{2}{3x}$$
$$(4\cdot3x)=(5\cdot2)$$
$$12x=10$$
$$x=\frac{5}{6}$$

If you have a fraction and a nonfraction, simply place a 1 under the nonfraction and *then* cross-multiply:

$$\frac{2x}{5}=4$$
$$\frac{2x}{5}=\frac{4}{1}$$
$$2x=20$$
$$x=10$$

This process of course is the same as multiplying both sides by the denominator:

$$\frac{2x}{5}=4$$
$$(5)\frac{2x}{5}=4(5)$$
$$\cancel{5}\frac{2x}{\cancel{5}}=20$$
$$x=10$$

PLAY

If $\frac{2a-1}{4b-1}=1$, which of the following is also true?

(A) $a=b$

(B) $a=2b$

(C) $2a=b$

(D) $2a=3b$

(E) $2a=3b$

Multiply both sides by the denominator and then simplify:

$$\frac{2a-1}{4b-1} = 1$$

$$\cancel{(4b-1)}\frac{2a-1}{\cancel{4b-1}} = 1(4b-1)$$

$$2a - 1 = 4b - 1$$

$$2a = 4b$$

$$a = 2b$$

The answer is (B).

Decimals

Working with decimals is simple with a few key points:

>> Line up the decimal points when adding or subtracting.

>> Count the decimal places when multiplying.

>> Move the decimal points of both numbers when dividing.

WARNING

Yes, you get an on-screen calculator, but don't rely on it. It's better to understand how the math works. Besides, I see *way* more typos on the calculator — which you're likely to miss — than mistakes on scratch paper — which you're likely to catch.

The following sections walk you through adding, subtracting, multiplying, and dividing decimals.

Adding and subtracting

To add or subtract decimals, first line up the decimal points. Then add or subtract as usual, placing the decimal point in the answer right below where it falls in the original numbers:

$$\begin{array}{r} 4.16 \\ +\,0.1 \\ \hline 4.26 \end{array}$$

Multiplying

When multiplying decimals, multiply the numbers first; then count the decimal spaces. Be sure that the number of decimal places in the answer is the same as the *total* number of decimal places in the numbers you're multiplying:

$$0.06 \times 0.03 = 0.0018$$

You know that 6×3 is 18. But the 0.06 and the 0.03 each has two decimal places, for a total of four. Therefore, the final answer also has four decimal places: 0.0018.

Here's a variation:

$$0.04 \times 0.05 = 0.0020$$

You know that 4×5 is 20, so be sure to include the entire 20 (two and zero) when counting the decimal places. After you have the decimal set correctly, you can drop the right-side zero, giving you 0.002.

PLAY

If a positive number with three decimal places is multiplied by another positive number with three decimal places, which of the following is the *least* product possible?

(A) 0.01

(B) 0.001

(C) 0.0001

(D) 0.00001

(E) 0.000001

For the least product possible, what is the smallest positive number with three decimal places? Probably 0.001. No, definitely 0.001. Anyway, you have two of these numbers, so multiply them starting with the 1s, $1 \times 1 = 1$, and count the six decimal places for 0.000001. The answer is (E).

Dividing

To divide decimals, move the decimal points of both numbers to the right, the same number of spaces, until the denominator is a whole number.

A tricky $\dfrac{0.032}{0.008}$ becomes an easy $\dfrac{0032.}{0008.}$, or $\dfrac{32}{8}$, for a final answer of 4.

PLAY

Try this on for size:

$$\frac{0.012}{0.004} =$$

$\dfrac{0.012}{0.004}$ becomes $\dfrac{0012.}{0004.}$, or $\dfrac{12}{4}$, for a final answer of 3. For the other two,

See? You don't need a calculator.

REMEMBER

The same thing goes for large numbers with extra zeros on the right: Cancel them, which means moving the decimal point to the *left*, except that here, you don't see the decimal point:

$$\frac{18,000}{3,000} = \frac{18}{3} = 6$$

Percentages

A percentage is a fraction of 100 — hence the name *percent*. In this example, $24\% = \dfrac{24}{100} = \dfrac{6}{25}$

100% is 1, and anything over 100% is more than 1:

$$150\% = \frac{150}{100} = \frac{3}{2} = 1.5$$

The next section shows you how to work these conversions quickly.

Converting

To answer a percentage-based math question, depending on the question, it may be easier to convert the percentage to a decimal or fraction. You may need to convert it back to a percentage to put the answer in the right form, but that happens later. Start with this:

>> **To convert a percentage to a decimal:** Move the decimal point two places to the left and drop the % sign: $35\% = 0.35$ $6\% = 0.06$ $50\% = 0.5$ $3.33\% = 0.0333$

>> **To convert a decimal to a percentage:** Move the decimal point two places to the right and add the % sign: $0.32 = 32\%$ $0.185 = 18.5\%$ $0.05 = 5\%$

>> **To convert a percentage to a fraction:** Place the number over 100, drop the % sign, and reduce if possible: $50\% = \frac{50}{100} = \frac{1}{2}$ $125\% = \frac{125}{100} = \frac{5}{4}$ $4\% = \frac{4}{100} = \frac{1}{25}$

>> **To convert a fraction to a percentage:** Set the fraction equal to x over 100 and cross-multiply to find x. The x is your percentage. Set $\frac{27}{50}$ up as $\frac{27}{50} = \frac{x}{100}$.

Now cross-multiply to find x:

$$\frac{27}{50} = \frac{x}{100}$$
$$50x = 2,700$$
$$5x = 270$$
$$x = 54$$

The fraction equals 54%.

Calculating percentage of change

A question may ask for a percentage of change from an original amount. To find this change, use the following formula:

$$\text{Percent of change} = \frac{\text{Amount of change}}{\text{Original amount}}$$

Finding the percentage of change requires a few simple steps:

1. **Find the number that increased or decreased, and from this number, the *amount* of change.**

   If a baseball team won 25 games last year and 30 games this year, the amount of change is 5, because the baseball team won 5 more games this year than last. If a salesperson earned $10,000 last year and $8,000 this year, the amount of change is $2,000.

   The *amount* of change is always positive, whether the value has increased or decreased. The salesperson's amount of change is still $2,000 (not –$2,000): He simply earned $2,000 *less* than he did last year.

2. **Place the amount of change over the original amount.**

   If the team won 25 games last year and 30 games this year, the original amount is 25. If the salesperson earned $10,000 last year and $8,000 this year, the original amount is $10,000.

3. **Divide and write the answer as a percentage.**

   For the baseball team, $\frac{5}{25} = \frac{1}{5} = 20\%$. Divide 1 by 5 to get 0.20, move the decimal point two places to the right, and add the % sign to make it a percentage.

   For the **hapless** (meaning *unfortunate,* the opposite of *happy*) salesman, $\frac{2,000}{10,000} = \frac{20}{100} = 20\%$.

   Again, divide 20 by 100 to get 0.20, move the decimal point two places to the right, and add the % sign to make it a percentage.

PLAY

Last season, Coach Jamieson's baseball team won 50 games. This season, the team won 30 games. What was the percentage decrease?

(A) 10

(B) 20

(C) 30

(D) 40

(E) 50

The number of games that Coach Jamieson's team won decreased by 20 (from 50 to 30). Place the 20 over the original amount of 50 for a decrease of 40%. The correct answer is (D).

Factorials

The *factorial* is indicated by an exclamation point (!) and represents the product of integers up to and including a specific integer. 4!, which stands for "four factorial," is $4 \times 3 \times 2 \times 1$, which of course is 24. So $4! = 24$.

There are many variations of the factorial, but the GRE keeps it simple. Just know these:

» You won't see a fraction, decimal, or exponent factorial.

» The negative factorial is a non-real number, so you won't see that either.

» The zero factorial, also known as 0!, equals 1, just as 1! equals 1, so $0! = 1!$.

TIP

When simplifying a factorial, *multiply the numbers last.* Here's an example of how to simplify a factorial in a fraction:

$$\frac{10!}{8!}$$

Because $10! = 10 \times 9 \times 8 \times 7 \times 6 \times 5 \times 4 \times 3 \times 2 \times 1$ and $8! = 8 \times 7 \times 6 \times 5 \times 4 \times 3 \times 2 \times 1$, cancel the matching numbers first:

$$\frac{10 \times 9 \times \cancel{8!}}{\cancel{8!}}$$

Then multiply: $10 \times 9 = 90$.

It wouldn't be beneath the GRE to present something like this:

$$\frac{100!}{98!}$$

Instead of panicking like the test-taker next to you who didn't read *GRE Prep 2023 For Dummies,* you can laugh out loud (well, not *too* loud, because you want to be kind) and heartily slash apart the fraction:

$$\frac{100 \times 99 \times \cancel{98!}}{\cancel{98!}}$$

This is why you multiply the numbers *last*: $100 \times 99 = 9,900$. See? You *don't* need the calculator.

Ratios

A *ratio* is a relationship between two similar numbers or quantities. A ratio acts like a fraction, written as either dogs : cats or $\frac{dogs}{cats}$. Here are a couple of examples:

> » The ratio *of* umbrellas *to* people is $\frac{umbrellas}{people}$.
>
> » The ratio *of* yachts *to* sailboats is yachts : sailboats.

When you know the tricks, ratios are some of the easiest problems to answer quickly. The following sections show you two ways to solve simple ratios and the best way to handle combined ratios.

Working with total numbers

Because ratios compare two amounts, the *total* number of items is a multiple of the sum of the numbers in the ratio. In other words, if the ratio is 3 dogs for every 2 cats, the total number of animals has to be a multiple of 5, such as 5, 10, or 15.

Try these exercises.

PLAY

At last night's game, the ratio of your team's fans to the other team's fans was 4 : 5. Which of the following *could* be the total number of fans at the game?

(A) 8

(B) 12

(C) 16

(D) 25

(E) 54

To solve this ratio problem, first add the numbers in the ratio: $4 + 5 = 9$. The total number of fans must be a multiple of 9 (9, 18, 27, 36, and so on). Can the total, for example, be 54? Yes, because 9 goes evenly into 54. Can it be 12? No, because 9 doesn't go evenly into 12. The correct answer is (E).

TIP

These GRE-style questions ask for numbers that *could* be true. But the GRE also asks for numbers that *must* be true or *cannot* be true. Be sure to double-check when selecting your answer, *especially* for questions with more than one answer.

Working with amounts in the ratio

Suppose that you're given a ratio and a total and are asked to find an amount in the ratio. The ratio of doughnut holes to doughnuts is 5 : 3, and there are 32 total snacks. How many doughnut holes are there? One way to find the answer is the following:

1. **Add the numbers in the ratio.**

   There are 5 doughnut holes for every 3 doughnuts, so $5 + 3 = 8$.

2. **Divide the total number of items by that sum.**

   There are 32 items total, so $\frac{32}{8} = 4$.

3. **Multiply the result from Step 2 by each term in the ratio.**

   Multiply 4 by 5 for 20 doughnut holes and 4 by 3 for 12 doughnuts.

4. **Add the answers to make sure that they match the total.**

Make sure that the 20 doughnut holes and 12 doughnuts total 32 items, which they do.

You can also set up the solution with this equation:

$$5x + 3x = 32$$
$$8x = 32$$
$$x = 4$$

And place 4 for x back in the equation:

$$5(4) + 3(4) = 32$$
$$20 + 12 = 32$$

There you have it: 20 doughnut holes and 12 doughnuts. Nice! Have some coffee.

With practice, this technique becomes second nature.

Maintaining the ratio

If the GRE math problem has a ratio, and you have to change the number of items while maintaining the ratio, you can calculate the number of items you need by setting the two ratios equal. Make the existing ratio (as a fraction) equal the new items (also as a fraction), and cross-multiply to find the missing value.

PLAY

Your college has to maintain its current ratio of 3 graduate assistants for every 40 students. If 240 new students are expected this fall, how many new graduate assistants does the school need to hire to maintain the ratio?

Solve the problem as follows:

1. **Set up the existing ratio as a fraction:**

$$\frac{\text{Assistants}}{\text{Students}} = \frac{3}{40}$$

2. **Set up the new additions as a fraction, with x as the unknown value:**

$$\frac{\text{Needed Assistants}}{\text{New Students}} = \frac{x}{240}$$

3. **Set the fractions equal:**

$$\frac{3}{40} = \frac{x}{240}$$

4. **Cross-multiply to solve for x.**

Multiply the numerator of each fraction by the denominator of the other:

$$40x = 720$$
$$4x = 72$$
$$x = 18$$

Thus, 18 new graduate assistants are needed to maintain the ratio.

Combining ratios

Sometimes, the GRE provides two separate ratios that have a common item. You can use that common item to combine the ratios for a single three-part ratio.

TIP

Combining ratios is a little like adding fractions. When adding fractions, you find the lowest common denominator. When combining ratios, find the lowest multiple of the item they have in common, just like a common denominator. Here's how you do that:

PLAY

Sam's jazz shop has 6 saxophones for every 5 drum kits and 2 drum kits for every 3 trombones. What's the ratio of saxophones to trombones?

Solve the problem as follows:

1. **Set up the ratios as $A : B$.**

Place the item that the ratios have in common (drum kits) in a column.

Saxes		Drums	Trombones
6	:	5	
		2	: 3

2. **Find a common multiple of the item that these ratios have in common.**

In this instance, both ratios include drum kits. The least common multiple of 5 and 2 (the numbers of drum kits) is 10.

3. **Multiply each ratio term so the quantity of the common item equals the common multiple (from Step 2).**

Find the common ratio exactly as though you were adding fractions, with drum kits as the common denominator:

$$\frac{6}{5} + \frac{3}{2} = \frac{6(2)}{5(2)} + \frac{3(5)}{2(5)} = \frac{12}{10} + \frac{15}{10}$$

You aren't adding fractions, of course, but you treat the ratios the same way. You want the number of drum kits to equal 10. Multiply both terms in the first ratio by 2, and multiply both terms in the second ratio by 5.

Saxes		Drums	Trombones
6(2)	:	5(2)	
		2(5)	: 3(5)

Saxes		Drums	Trombones
12	:	10	
		10	: 15

4. **Write out a combined ratio.**

The combined ratio of saxophones to drum kits to trombones is $12 : 10 : 15$. To answer the question, give only the ratio of saxophones to trombones, which is $12 : 15$, or $4 : 5$.

Solving Algebra and Functions

Algebra and functions use letters and abstract operations to represent mathematics to solve for an unknown value, usually represented by x. You probably solved algebra in junior high and high school, and perhaps even in college, but here's a refresher on the details that may have escaped over time, in the context of the GRE.

Bases and exponents

When you multiply a number repeatedly by itself, you raise that number to a certain power. Here's an example: 3 to the power of 4, or 3^4, is $3 \times 3 \times 3 \times 3 = 81$. In this example, 3 is the base, and 4 is the exponent. The *exponent* simply tells you how many times to multiply the *base* (number) by itself. Here are a few more examples:

» $10^2 = 10 \times 10 = 100$

» $x^4 = x \cdot x \cdot x \cdot x$

Remember these rules of bases and exponents:

Any number to the zero power equals 1:

$$x^0 = 1 \qquad 5^0 = 1 \qquad 129^0 = 1$$

Any number to a negative exponent is the reciprocal of that number to its positive exponent:

$$y^{-4} = \frac{1}{y^4} \qquad 6^{-3} = \frac{1}{6^3} \qquad 325^{-1} = \frac{1}{325}$$

REMEMBER

A number with a negative exponent isn't negative. When you flip it, you get the reciprocal, and the negative goes away:

$$5^{-3} = \frac{1}{5^3} = \frac{1}{125}$$

When you raise 10 to a power, you get 1 followed by the number of zeros equal to that power:

» $10^2 = 100$ (two zeros)

» $10^4 = 10,000$ (four zeros)

Because $10^4 = 10,000$, 5×10^4 is $5 \times 10,000$, which equals 50,000.

To multiply like bases, add the exponents:

» $(x^3)(x^2) = x^{(3+2)} = x^5$

» $5^3 \times 5^4 = 5^{(3+4)} = 5^7$

WARNING

You can't multiply *different* bases. $x^2 \cdot y^3$ stays $x^2 \cdot y^3$, and $14^3 \times 15^5$ stays $14^3 \times 15^5$.

To divide like bases, subtract the exponents:

» $x^5 \div x^3 = x^{(5-3)} = x^2$

» $\dfrac{5^8}{5^4} = 5^{(8-4)} = 5^4$

Multiply the exponents of a base inside and outside parentheses:

» $(x^2)^3 = x^{(2 \times 3)} = x^6$

» $(175^0)^3 = 175^{(0 \times 3)} = 175^0 = 1$

REMEMBER

This rule is true even with negative exponents:

>> $\left(x^{-2}\right)^{3} = x^{(-2\times3)} = x^{-6}$

>> $\left(x^{-2}\right)^{-4} = x^{(-2\times-4)} = x^{8}$

To add or subtract like bases with like powers, add or subtract the numerical coefficients of the bases.

The *numerical coefficient* is the number to the left of the base. In $15y^{2}$, y is the base, and 15 is the numerical coefficient. Note that the exponent 2 applies only to the y, not the whole $15y$. To subtract:

$$15y^{2} - 10y^{2}$$
$$(15-10)y^{2}$$
$$5y^{2}$$

Try this Quantitative Comparison (QC) question with bases and exponents. (In a QC question, you compare the contents in two columns.)

PLAY

Quantity A	Quantity B
x^{3}	$\dfrac{x^{7}}{x^{4}}$

(A) Quantity A is greater.

(B) Quantity B is greater.

(C) The two quantities are equal.

(D) The relationship cannot be determined from the information given.

Remember that when you divide, you subtract the exponents, so $x^{(7-4)} = x^{3}$, regardless of the value of x. The correct answer is (C).

Math operators

You see a problem with a strange symbol — a triangle, a star, or a circle with a dot, as in the following example. You've never seen it before, and you're not sure what it means. It's probably a math operator, such as $+$, $-$, $\times$, or $\div$, but it's a new one that the GRE uses just for this one math question. Don't worry — the GRE always tells you what the symbol means (or sets up the question so you can figure it out).

The approach is simple: Place a number for the variable. The math itself is *always* easy. The trick is knowing how to set up the equation.

The symbol may be part of an equation, like this:

$$a \odot b \odot c = \frac{(a+b)}{(b+c)}$$

A question follows the explanation, like this:

$$3 \odot 4 \odot 5 =$$

Here's how you solve it:

1. **Substitute the numbers for the letters.**

   For this problem, substitute 3, 4, and 5 for *a*, *b*, and *c*, respectively:

   $$3 \odot 4 \odot 5 = \frac{(3+4)}{(4+5)}$$

2. **Solve the equation:**

   $$\frac{3+4}{4+5} = \frac{7}{9}$$

The GRE keeps things interesting with variations like this:

PLAY

$$\text{If } [[x]] = \frac{2x}{x+2}, \text{ then } [[-4]] =$$

To solve, substitute −4 for *x*:

$$[[-4]] = \frac{2(-4)}{(-4)+2}$$

Then solve the equation for your answer:

$$\frac{2(-4)}{(-4)+2} = \frac{-8}{-2} = 4$$

Solving for X

Solving for *x* is just that: turning something like $2x + 3 = 5$ into $2x = 2$ and finally $x = 1$. Simple, right? But the GRE, being what it is, varies this idea in ways you haven't seen since your SAT or ACT and you won't see again until your kids need help with their SATs. But that's another story.

The GRE, still being what it is, stays within its scope of math topics and sets the questions up for easy answering if you know how to answer them. This section takes you through these GRE-level topics and shows you how to answer each question in less than a minute.

Solving for x with a number

To solve for *x* or any other variable that the question asks for, move that variable to one side of the equation, and divide both sides of the equation by the coefficient. Where $4x = x + 6$, subtract *x* from both sides of the equation for $3x = 6$. Divide both sides by 3, for $x = 2$, and the solution is 2.

TIP

GRE algebra questions are typically simple to solve, but once in a while, there's a question where it's easier to try the answer choices. Always go for solving the problem first, but if that seems to be tricky, trying out answers may be the way to go.

PLAY

Solve for *x*:

$$5^{\frac{x}{5}} + \frac{x}{2} = 30$$

(A) 7

(B) 8

(C) 10

(D) 12

(E) 14

You *could* solve for x, but I wouldn't. Instead, start with the answer choice number that's easiest to work with, in this case probably 10. Then the process goes like this:

$$5^{\frac{(10)}{5}} + \frac{(10)}{2} = 30$$
$$5^2 + 5 = 30$$
$$25 + 5 = 30$$

See? Almost too easy. Solving for x would have been a nightmare, but this way it's an easy $x = 10$. Correct answer: (C).

Solving with the FOIL method

When you're multiplying any number by a *binomial* (two numbers in parentheses), use the *distributive property*, which means multiplying all the values inside the parentheses by the number to the left of the parentheses. Here's an example:

$$9(3x + 2y)$$
$$9(3x) + 9(2y)$$
$$27x + 18y$$

When you're multiplying two binomials, such as $(a + b)(a - b)$, you basically multiply everything in one set of parentheses by everything in the other set of parentheses and then add up all the results. This technique is also known as the *FOIL method*, which stands for *First, Outer, Inner, Last*. Try it with the equation $(a + b)(a - b)$

1. **Multiply the *First* variables:** $a \times a = a^2$

2. **Multiply the *Outer* variables:** $a \times (-b) = -ab$

3. **Multiply the *Inner* variables:**

   $b \times a = ba$ (which is the same as ab).

4. **Multiply the *Last* variables:** $b \times (-b) = -b^2$

5. **Combine like terms:**

   $a^2 - ab + ab - b^2$ (Here, the $-ab$ and $+ab$ cancel out.)
   $a^2 - b^2$

Like terms are two or more terms with the same variable(s) and exponent. $3x^3$ and $2x^3$ are like terms, and you may combine them as follows: $3x^3 + 2x^3 = 5x^3$. You can't combine $3x^3$ and $3y^3$ because the variables differ, nor $3x^3$ and $3x^5$ because the exponents differ.

REMEMBER

When you're multiplying, the order doesn't matter, as in $5 \times 3 = 3 \times 5$ and $ab = ba$.

Try the following FOIL-based question. The secret is to do what you can. You can FOIL the expressions, so start with that:

PLAY

If $(x + 3y)(x - 3y) = 10$, what is the value of $x^2 - 9y^2$?

(A) 5

(B) 10

(C) 15

(D) 20

(E) 25

Don't get stuck. FOIL it:

$$(x + 3y)(x - 3y) = 10$$
$$x^2 - 3xy + 3xy - 9y^2 = 10$$
$$x^2 - 9y^2 = 10$$

That's it? I mean, that's it! The answer is (B).

Factoring back out

As often as you FOIL on the GRE, you also *factor*, which is the opposite of FOILing. Factoring takes an algebraic expression from its final form back to its original form of two binomials. You perform this operation when an equation contains x^2 to find the two possible values of *x*.

REMEMBER

x (or any letter in the equation) always has *one* value. Most equations with an *x* squared have two *possible* values for *x*, but *x* actually has one value. If $x^2 = 25$, you know that *x* equals 5 *or* −5, but *not* both. If $y^2 = 9$, the two *possible* solutions are 3 and −3, but the *value* of *y* is *either* 3 *or* −3. These possible values of *x* or *y* are also called the *solutions* or the *roots* of the equation.

TIP

When solving for x^2, also known as a *quadratic equation* (though you won't need the quadratic formula, so put that right back on the shelf), the first thing to do is set the equation equal to zero. If the GRE gives you $48 = x^2 + 2x$, make it $x^2 + 2x - 48 = 0$. If the exam gives you $20 = h^2 - h$, don't think about it; make it $h^2 - h - 20 = 0$.

Given $x^2 - 4x - 12 = 0$, what are the two possible values of *x*? Factor the answer one step at a time:

1. **Draw two sets of parentheses:**

$$(\quad)(\quad) = 0$$

2. **Fill in the *First* terms.**

To get x^2, the *first* terms have to be *x* and *x:*

$$(x\quad)(x\quad) = 0$$

3. **Fill in the *Last* terms.**

You need two numbers that equal −12 when multiplied and −4 when added. Start with the multiplied number, in this case −12: You have 3×4, 2×6, and 1×12. Keep in mind that one of these terms is negative, for the −12, so which two numbers add up to −4? After a few tries, you find that −6 and +2 do the trick. Multiplied, they equal −12, and added, they equal −4. Now you can complete the equation:

$$(x - 6)(x + 2) = 0$$

REMEMBER

Whether you write it as $(x - 6)(x + 2)$ or $(x + 2)(x - 6)$ doesn't matter. These expressions are multiplied, so they can be in either order.

Now solve for *x* as two separate equations: $(x - 6) = 0$ and $(x + 2) = 0$, for *x* values of 6 and − 2. Remember that *x* doesn't equal *both* 6 and −2; it equals one *or* the other. That's why the question is phrased "What are the two *possible* values for *x*?"

Square roots and radicals

You're likely to see math problems on the GRE that include square roots or radicals. A *square root* is a number that's multiplied by itself for a result. 3 is the square root of 9, because $3 \times 3 = 9$. A *radical* is another way of expressing a square root. The square root of 9 may be represented as $\sqrt{9}$. Though higher-level roots exist in math, the *square* root is the root you most commonly see on the GRE.

REMEMBER

A square root can be on only a *positive* number, such as $\sqrt{25}$, and never $\sqrt{-25}$, because a negative number multiplied by itself results in a positive answer. If you see a square root on a negative number, then this number isn't real, which means that the equation with the number won't work. $\sqrt{-25}$ isn't -5, because the square root is from the *same* number multiplied by itself (squared), and -5 times itself is $+25$.

The following sections review the math problems you may encounter on the exam related to roots and radicals. But first, you need to know how to simplify them.

Simplifying

When possible, simplify radicals to get rid of them. *Simplifying* basically means reducing the radical to its most manageable form, often getting rid of the radical. To simplify a radical, factor the number inside and pull out pairs of factors. Here are a few examples:

» $\sqrt{1} = \sqrt{1 \times 1} = 1$
» $\sqrt{4} = \sqrt{2 \times 2} = 2$
» $\sqrt{9} = \sqrt{3 \times 3} = 3$

In some cases, part of the radical remains, but you can still reduce it to make the number easier to work with. In these problems, the GRE simply expects you to reduce the radical as far as you can, and the correct answer will typically include a radical. Here's an example of a radical that you can't reduce to an integer but can simplify:

$$\sqrt{300} = \sqrt{10 \times 10 \times 3}$$
$$= \sqrt{10 \times 10} \times \sqrt{3}$$
$$= 10 \times \sqrt{3}$$
$$= 10\sqrt{3}$$

In this example, the square root of 100 is 10, so the 10 comes out of the radical. The 3, however, stays inside the radical, and the two numbers (10 and $\sqrt{3}$) are multiplied for a result of $10\sqrt{3}$. The answer choice will typically look like $10\sqrt{3}$, and you won't have to estimate the value.

To take the square root of a fraction, such as $\sqrt{\frac{9}{25}}$, take the roots of the top and bottom separately. You know that $\sqrt{9} = 3$ and $\sqrt{25} = 5$, so $\sqrt{\frac{9}{25}} = \frac{\sqrt{9}}{\sqrt{25}} = \frac{3}{5}$.

PLAY

If $a = \sqrt{\frac{1}{16}}$, what is the value of $\sqrt{a}$?

(A) $\frac{1}{16}$

(B) $\frac{1}{8}$

(C) $\frac{1}{4}$

(D) $\frac{1}{2}$

(E) 1

Start with the value of a:

$$a = \sqrt{\frac{1}{16}}$$

$$= \frac{1}{4}$$

Take the square root of that:

$$\sqrt{a} = \sqrt{\frac{1}{4}}$$

$$= \frac{1}{2}$$

There you have it, for answer (D).

Adding and subtracting

To add and subtract numbers with radicals, stick with these rules:

REMEMBER

» **You can add or subtract *similar* radicals.** Just add or subtract the number in front of the radical: $2\sqrt{7} + 3\sqrt{7} = 5\sqrt{7}$ $4\sqrt{5} - \sqrt{5} = 3\sqrt{5}$

This works just like adding or subtracting numbers with x: $2x + 3x = 5x$ and $4y - y = 3y$.

» **You *can't* add or subtract *different* radicals.** $6\sqrt{5} + 4\sqrt{3}$ stays the same, just as $4x + 5y$ stays the same.

If the radicals aren't similar, you may still be able to add or subtract them. Try to simplify one radical to make it similar to the other:

$$\sqrt{28} + \sqrt{7} =$$
$$\sqrt{4 \times 7} + \sqrt{7} =$$
$$2\sqrt{7} + \sqrt{7} = 3\sqrt{7}$$

PLAY

Try this problem:

$$\sqrt{27} + 5\sqrt{12} =$$

Here is the answer:

$$\sqrt{27} + 5\sqrt{12} =$$
$$\sqrt{3 \times 3 \times 3} + 5\sqrt{2 \times 2 \times 3} =$$
$$3\sqrt{3} + \left(5 \times 2\sqrt{3}\right) =$$
$$3\sqrt{3} + 10\sqrt{3} = 13\sqrt{3}$$

Multiplying and dividing

To multiply and divide numbers with radicals, follow these rules:

» **Put all the numbers inside one radical and then multiply or divide the numbers:**

$$\sqrt{5} \times \sqrt{6} \rightarrow \sqrt{5 \times 6} = \sqrt{30}$$

$$\frac{\sqrt{15}}{\sqrt{5}} \rightarrow \sqrt{\frac{15}{5}} = \sqrt{3}$$

» **If numbers are in front of the radicals, multiply or divide them separately.** Because the order doesn't matter when multiplying, move the pieces around to make them easier to multiply.

$$6\sqrt{3} \times 4\sqrt{2} \rightarrow (6 \times 4)\left(\sqrt{3} \times \sqrt{2}\right)$$
$$= (24)\left(\sqrt{6}\right)$$
$$= 24\sqrt{6}$$

Dividing works pretty much the same way. Divide the numbers in front of the radicals separately from the radicals themselves:

$$6\sqrt{10} \div 2\sqrt{5} \rightarrow (6 \div 2)(\sqrt{10 \div 5})$$
$$= (3)(\sqrt{2})$$
$$= 3\sqrt{2}$$

PLAY

$7\sqrt{5} \times 3\sqrt{6} =$

(A) $10\sqrt{11}$

(B) $10\sqrt{30}$

(C) $21\sqrt{11}$

(D) $21\sqrt{30}$

(E) 630

You know that $7 \times 3 = 21$ and $\sqrt{5} \times \sqrt{6} = \sqrt{30}$, so the answer is $21\sqrt{30}$. This one is straight multiplication. The correct answer is (D).

Simplifying first

If you can simplify what's under the radical, do that first; then take the square root of the answer. Here's an example:

$$\sqrt{\frac{1}{3} + \frac{1}{9}}$$

First, simplify the fractions: $\frac{1}{3} + \frac{1}{9} = \frac{4}{9}$. Next, take the square roots of the top and bottom separately:

$$\sqrt{\frac{4}{9}} = \frac{\sqrt{4}}{\sqrt{9}} = \frac{2}{3}$$

And the answer is $\frac{2}{3}$.

Coordinate geometry

Coordinate geometry is where algebra and geometry meet — a method of describing points, lines, and shapes with algebra. It all happens on a grid known as the *coordinate plane*.

The coordinate plane, also known as the *xy rectangular grid* or *xy plane*, is a two-dimensional area defined by a horizontal *x*-axis and a vertical *y*-axis that intersect at a *point of origin* labeled (0, 0). Each point is labeled using an *ordered pair* (*x, y*) with the first number in the parentheses indicating how far to the right or left of (0, 0) the point is and the second number indicating how far above or below (0, 0) the point is. This point has an *x*-value of 2 and a *y*-value of 1, for the coordinates (2, 1):

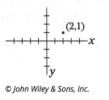

© John Wiley & Sons, Inc.

Here's what you need for the coordinate geometry questions on the GRE.

Common problems

Most questions on coordinate geometry involve the *linear equation*, thoroughly explored in the following sections. Before you get there, however, here are other common coordinate geometry topics you need to review on a site like Khan Academy (www.khanacademy.org) as you study for the GRE.

> » **Distance between two points:** To find the distance between two points on the grid, you can use the *distance formula,* which is based on the Pythagorean theorem.

> » **Slope of a line:** The *slope of a line* can be found with "rise over run," which refers to the distance that a segment of the line moves vertically (its "rise") divided by the distance it moves horizontally (its "run").

> » **Midpoint formula:** To find the midpoint of a line segment defined by the coordinates of two points on the graph, you can use the *midpoint formula:*
>
> $$\text{midpoint} = \left(\frac{x_1 + x_2}{2}, \frac{y_1 + y_2}{2} \right)$$

Linear equations

A *linear equation* is any equation with two letters, usually x and y, and no exponents, such as $2x + y = 5$. The *slope-intercept* form shows it as solved for y, such as $y = -2x + 5$, or $y = mx + b$. This form is called *slope-intercept* because it shows the slope and y-intercept right there in the equation: m is the slope, and b is the y-intercept (the point at which the line representing the equation intersects the y-axis).

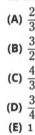

PLAY

In the xy-coordinate grid, which is the slope of the line with the equation $2y - 3x = 6$?

(A) $\dfrac{2}{3}$

(B) $\dfrac{3}{2}$

(C) $\dfrac{4}{3}$

(D) $\dfrac{3}{4}$

(E) 1

Convert the equation $2y - 3x = 6$ to its *slope-intercept* form, which means that you solve for y. Then the x-coefficient is the slope of the line:

$$2y - 3x = 6$$
$$2y = 3x + 6$$
$$y = \frac{3x}{2} + 3$$

The answer is (B).

Questions on the GRE that involve the slope-intercept form may provide the coordinates of a point through which the line passes and require you to calculate the y-intercept. The line

$y = 7x + b$ passes through point $(4, 15)$. At what point does the line cross the y-axis? To get the answer, place 4 for x and 15 for y and then solve the equation:

$$y = 7x + b$$
$$(15) = 7(4) + b$$
$$15 = 28 + b$$
$$15 - 28 = b$$
$$b = -13$$

So the line crosses the y-axis at the point $(0, -13)$.

You can also use the slope-intercept form to find the slope of a line when given its y-intercept and the coordinates of any point on the line. Suppose that a line crosses the y-axis at $y = 5$ and goes through the point $(4, 13)$, and you need to determine its slope. Simply place the given values in the slope-intercept form:

$$y = mx + b$$
$$(13) = m(4) + (5)$$
$$13 - 5 = 4m$$
$$8 = 4m$$
$$m = 2$$

Given the equation $2x + 3y = 24$, find an ordered pair (the x-y coordinates of a point) that makes the equation true. To test this, place in values for x and y, and make sure the equation works. In this case, the ordered pairs $(0, 8)$, $(6, 4)$, and $(-3, 10)$ make the equation true.

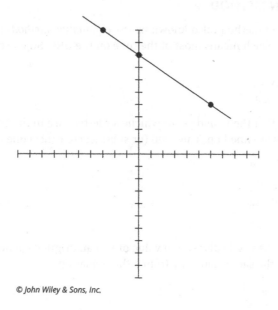

PLAY

Identify the (x, y) coordinates that make the equation $5x + 3y = 27$ true.

Select all correct answers.

(A) $(0, 9)$

(B) $(6, 1)$

(C) $(9, -6)$

(D) $(5, 2)$

(E) $(6, -1)$

(F) $(3, -2)$

To solve this problem, substitute the x and y values of each answer into $5x + 3y = 27$, and see which ones make the equation equal to 27:

A	$5(0) + 3(9) = 0 + 27 = 27$	Yes
B	$5(6) + 3(1) = 30 + 3 = 33$	No
C	$5(9) + 3(-6) = 45 - 18 = 27$	Yes
D	$5(5) + 3(2) = 25 + 6 = 31$	No
E	$5(6) + 3(-1) = 30 - 3 = 27$	Yes
F	$5(3) + 3(-2) = 15 - 6 = 9$	No

The correct answers are (A), (C), and (E).

Two linear equations

Any linear equation has endless solutions, because for each value of x, there's a corresponding value of y. With *two* linear equations, also called *simultaneous equations,* the equations usually depict lines that cross, which means there is a single set of x and y values where the lines cross. These single values for x and y are called the *solutions* to the equation. There are two ways to find these solutions: addition and substitution.

ADDITION METHOD

The addition method (also known as the *elimination method*) is easy and works best for simpler equations, which means most of the time on the GRE. Suppose that you're solving this problem:

PLAY

$$5x - 2y = 4$$
$$x + 2y = 8$$

Make sure that the xs and ys (or whichever letters are in the equations), the numbers, and the equal signs are lined up. Then add (or subtract) to cancel one unknown and solve for the other:

$$\begin{array}{r} 5x - 2y = 4 \\ + x + 2y = 8 \\ \hline 6x + 0 = 12 \\ x = 2 \end{array}$$

Now place the newly discovered value of x in an original equation to find the value of y. You should get the same value of y from either equation:

$$5(2) - 2y = 4$$
$$10 - 2y = 4$$
$$-2y = -6$$
$$y = 3$$

If you were to graph the two equations, the lines would meet at $(2,3)$.

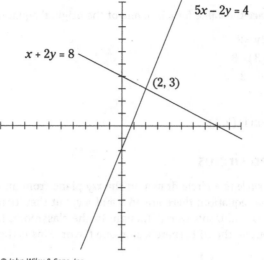

© John Wiley & Sons, Inc.

SUBSTITUTION METHOD

The other method is substitution, which has more steps but works better for some complicated equations. Just follow these steps:

1. In one equation, solve for the first unknown in terms of the second unknown.

2. Substitute the result from Step 1 for the first unknown in the other equation and solve for the second unknown.

3. Place the value for the second unknown into either equation, and solve for the first unknown.

It's easier than it sounds. Try this example:

$$5x - 2y = 4$$
$$x + 2y = 8$$

In this example, the second equation is simpler, so start with that. Solve for x in terms of y:

$$x + 2y = 8$$
$$x = 8 - 2y$$

Now substitute $8 - 2y$ for x in the first equation and solve for y:

$$5(8 - 2y) - 2y = 4$$
$$40 - 10y - 2y = 4$$
$$-12y = 4 - 40$$
$$-12y = -36$$
$$y = 3$$

Finally, place the value for *y* into one of the original equations to find the value of *x*:

$$x + 2y = 8$$
$$x + 2(3) = 8$$
$$x + 6 = 8$$
$$x = 2$$

The solution is $(2, 3)$.

Graphed circles

A *graphed circle* is a circle drawn on the *x/y* plane from an equation. The equation is like a contorted linear equation; there are an *x* and a *y*, but they're twisted and squared instead of a nice, simple equation. Don't worry, though. In the classroom, the teachers vary the heck out of this concept, but on the GRE, there's only one flavor. This is the equation for the graphed circle:

$$(x - h)^2 + (y - k)^2 = r^2$$

In this equation, *h* and *k* are the *x* and *y* values of the center, and *r* is the radius. The way you remember is that the *x* and *y* values of the center become negative (or positive, if they're already negative), and the radius is squared. Suppose that you have a circle in which the (x, y) coordinates of the center are $(3, -2)$ and the radius is 5.

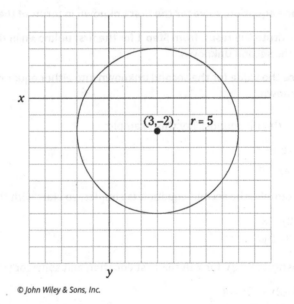

© John Wiley & Sons, Inc.

Thus, the equation of this circle is $(x - 3)^2 + (y + 2)^2 = 5^2$. It also may appear as $(x - 3)^2 + (y + 2)^2 = 25$, but the radius is still 5.

A circle is drawn in the *x/y* coordinate grid. If the radius is 3 and the (x, y) coordinates of the center are $(-2.5, 0.5)$, which of the following is the equation for the circle?

(A) $(x + 2.5)^2 + (y - 0.5)^2 = 3$

(B) $(x - 2.5)^2 - (y + 0.5)^2 = 3$

(C) $(x - 2.5)^2 + (y + 0.5)^2 = 3^2$

(D) $(x + 2.5)^2 - (y - 0.5)^2 = 3^2$

(E) $(x + 2.5)^2 + (y - 0.5)^2 = 3^2$

Knowing the equation of the circle is $(x-h)^2+(y-k)^2=r^2$, just place -2.5 for x, 0.5 for y, and 3 for r, like this:

$$(x-h)^2+(y-k)^2=r^2$$
$$(x-(-2.5))^2+(y-(0.5))^2=(3)^2$$
$$(x+2.5)^2+(y-0.5)^2=3^2$$

Watch out for trap answers in which x and y have the wrong sign or r isn't squared. Correct answer: (E).

Patterns in a sequence

A GRE sequence question has you interpret a numeric pattern from an equation. The term is indicated by a letter, such as a, and counted with a subscript number, such as: $a_1, a_2, a_3, a_4, a_5, ..., a_n$.

You're typically given one value for a, such as $a_1 = 10$. The 1 in a_1 means "the *first a*," and the statement tells you that the first a has a value of 10. Be sure not to confuse the subscript number, in this case the 1 in a_1, with the value of that particular a, in this case 10.

Next, you're given an equation that describes the relationship between the sequential terms — in other words, the value of the next a, such as $a_{n+1} = a_n + 3$

Though the value of n (the subscript of a) changes, it has only one value at a time in the equation. If $n = 1$, $= n + 1 = 2$. Thus, the equation can be rewritten as $a_2 = a_1 + 3$.

Don't get caught up in the math. Under all that subscript, what it tells you is simple. The *next a* is 3 more than the *previous a*. The second a, which is a_2, is 3 more than the first a, which is a_1.

The next iteration of the equation, with 1 added to n again, looks like this:

$$a_3 = a_2 + 3$$

It tells you that the *third a*, a_3, is 3 more than the *second a*, a_2. In other words, if $a_1 = 10$, then $a_2 = 13$, $a_3 = 16$, and so forth. That's the pattern, and the question is based on this pattern, such as "What is the value of a_6?" Just keep adding 3 until you reach the sixth a:

$$a_1 = 10$$
$$a_2 = 13$$
$$a_3 = 16$$
$$a_4 = 19$$
$$a_5 = 22$$
$$a_6 = 25$$

PLAY

In the sequence $b_{n+1} = b_n - 4$, for all integers b and n, where $b_3 = 12$, what is the value of b_5?

(A) 20

(B) 16

(C) 8

(D) 4

(E) 0

Start with the equation $b_{n+1} = b_n - 4$, which translates to English as "The *next b* is 4 less than *this b*." If *this b*, or b_3, is 12, then the *next b*, b_4 is 8, and b_5 is 4. Correct answer: (D).

Solving f(x) functions

A *function* is a graphed equation, such as $y = 2x + 3$. Instead of y, however, there's an $f(x)$, like this: $f(x) = 2x + 3$. The $f(x)$ represents the resulting y value, and you place a value for x by substituting the number in the $f(x)$. If $x = 5$, $f(5) = 2(5) + 3$, and $f(5) = 13$. Note that the function may use other letters, such as $g(h)$.

Sometimes the $f(x)$ question is easier to solve by trying out the answer choices.

TIP

Questions on the GRE that involve $f(x)$ typically give you an equation where you place the values for x for the answer. Here's how you get started:

1. **Place the value of x from the $f(x)$ into each x in the equation.**
2. **Watch for variations in the $f(x)$ or the equation.**

Plenty of these are on the GRE, so here are some examples of variations:

$f(x) = (2x)^3$. Solve for $f(2)$.

To solve, substitute the number in parentheses for the letter in parentheses (in this case, place in 2 for x):

PLAY

$$f(2) = (2(2))^3 = 4^3 = 64$$

Try another one:

When $f(x) = x^2 + 2x$, what is the value of $2f(5)$?

First find the value of $f(5)$:

PLAY

$$f(x) = x^2 + 2x$$
$$f(5) = (5)^2 + 2(5)$$
$$= 25 + 10$$
$$= 35$$

Now that you know what $f(5)$ is, double it for $2f(5)$:

$$f(5) = 35$$
$$2f(5) = 70$$

See, the math is *always* simple but it *looks* menacing. Just remember that there's always a simple trick, but it helps if you've seen it before and know what to do — and practice.

Drawing Geometry

GRE geometry is all about basic shapes that you know and understand, along with familiar details that need refreshing but come back to you in no time. As with all GRE math, you could see a specific scope of topics see (such as parts of a circle), and outside that scope are topics that you aren't likely to see (such as cones and spheres). This chapter covers the topics you need to understand and gives you hands-on practice answering sample questions.

Lines and angles

The main parts of most of these shapes are lines and angles.

REMEMBER

GRE images are *typically* drawn to scale, well enough for you to get a sense of what's going on in the drawing. The drawing or the description will always tell you everything that you need (such as side lengths, parallel sides, and right-angle boxes), so whether it's drawn to scale really doesn't matter. Always look in the description for clues to unravel the drawing. On that note, if the drawing has a label that reads, "Figure not drawn to scale," it's *way* off.

Lines

A *line* is straight and continuous. If it curves, it's not a line, and if it ends, it's a *segment* (running between two points) or a *ray* (going in only one direction, like an arrow). For the most part, don't worry about this distinction, but if you see these terms, you know what they are.

Parallel lines don't cross and are represented by the symbol ||. *Perpendicular lines* cross at right angles and are represented by the symbol ⊥ or in a drawing by the right-angle indicator ⌐. Find more on right angles in the next section. A *perpendicular bisector* is a line that passes through the midpoint of a line segment and is perpendicular to it.

Angles

An *angle* is the space between two lines or segments that cross or share an endpoint. Fortunately, there's not much to understanding angles when you know the types of angles and a few key concepts.

Finding an angle is usually a matter of simple addition or subtraction. Besides the rules in the following sections, these three rules apply to the angles on the GRE:

>> An angle can't be negative.

>> An angle can't be 0 degrees or 180 degrees.

>> Fractional angles are rare on the GRE. An angle is typically a whole number and rounded to be easy to work with.

A *right angle* equals 90 degrees and is represented by perpendicular lines with a small box where the two lines meet.

WARNING

Watch out for lines that appear to be perpendicular but really aren't. An angle is a right angle *only* if the description reads, "The lines (or segments) are perpendicular," you see the box in the angle, or you're told the shape is a square, rectangle, or right triangle. Otherwise, you can't assume that the angle is 90 degrees.

ℓ_2

ℓ_2 ——— **Right angle**

——— $a°$ | $b°$ ———
Not necessarily a right angle

© *John Wiley & Sons, Inc.*

TIP

Other than the words *right angle* and *bisect*, you probably won't see the following terms, so don't worry about memorizing words such as *obtuse* and *supplementary*. But review the definitions so that you understand how the angles work, because that's the key to solving almost any GRE angle problem.

>> An *acute angle* is any angle between 0 and 90 degrees.

>> An *obtuse angle* is any angle between 90 and 180 degrees.

>> *Complementary angles* add to 90 degrees to form a right angle.

>> *Supplementary angles* add to 180 degrees to form a straight line.

>> *Vertical angles* always have equal measures and are the resulting opposite angles when two lines cross.

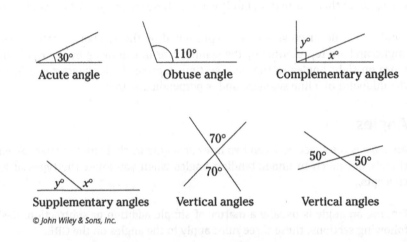

Acute angle   Obtuse angle   Complementary angles

Supplementary angles   Vertical angles   Vertical angles

© John Wiley & Sons, Inc.

A *bisector*, or line that bisects, cuts directly down the middle. You need to know this term. If a line (or segment) bisects an angle, it divides that angle into two equal angles; if a first segment bisects a second segment, the first one cuts the second one perfectly in half. And if the first segment bisects the second segment at 90 degrees, it's a *perpendicular bisector*, and yes, the GRE expects you to know that. Don't worry — there will almost always be a drawing.

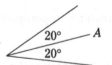

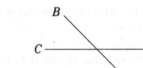

Segment *A* bisects the angle   Segment *B* bisects segment *C*

Segment *D* perpendicularly bisects segment *E*

© John Wiley & Sons, Inc.

Angles around a point total 360 degrees, just as in a circle.

360°

A line that cuts through two parallel lines forms two sets of four equal angles. In this drawing, all the *x*s are the same, and all the *y*s are the same.

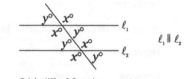

$\ell_1 \parallel \ell_2$

WARNING

Never assume that lines are parallel unless the question or image states that they are. The symbol $\ell_1 \parallel \ell_2$ indicates parallel lines.

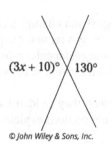

$(3x + 10)°$ 130°

PLAY

In the preceding figure, the value of *x* is

(A) 20

(B) 30

(C) 40

(D) 50

(E) 60

The opposite angles are *vertical*, meaning that they equal each other. Because the left-side angle equals the right-side angle, set up the equation like this:

$$(3x + 10)° = 130°$$
$$3x + 10 = 130$$
$$3x = 120$$
$$x = 40$$

The correct answer is (C). By the way, this is why you solve algebra before drawing geometry: Algebra is *patent* (apparent) throughout geometry.

Polygons

A *polygon* is any closed shape consisting of line segments, from a *triangle* (three sides) to a *dodecagon* (a dozen sides) and beyond. (Don't worry about knowing the dodecagon.) The polygons you're most likely going to encounter on the GRE are triangles and *quadrilaterals* (with four sides). Table 3-1 lists the names of polygons you may bump into, but don't get caught up with the names; these problems almost always include a drawing, so you can count the sides.

TABLE 3-1 **Polygons**

Number of Sides	Name
3	Triangle
4	Quadrilateral (including the square, rectangle, trapezoid, and parallelogram)
5	Pentagon
6	Hexagon (think of x in six and x in hex)
7	Heptagon
8	Octagon
9	Nonagon
10	Decagon

REMEMBER

A polygon with all sides equal and all angles equal is a *regular polygon*. An equilateral triangle is a regular triangle, and a square is a regular quadrilateral. *Equilateral* refers to equal side lengths, as in a diamond (rhombus), and *equiangular* refers to equal angles, as in a rectangle. With the equilateral triangle, the equal sides give it equal angles, but this isn't the case with other shapes.

If two polygons are *congruent*, they're identical. If they're *similar*, they have identical angles but different sizes. The following sections explain what you need to know about polygons for the GRE.

Measuring total interior angles

Because you may be asked to find the total interior angle measure of a particular polygon, keep this formula in mind (where *n* stands for the number of sides):

$$\text{Angle total} = (n-2)180°$$

For example, you calculate the sum of a triangle's interior angles like this:

$$(3-2)180° = 1 \times 180° = 180°$$

TIP

If you can't remember the formula, start with a triangle, where three sides have an angle total of 180°, and add 180 for each additional side.

Measuring one interior angle

I've seen GRE problems asking for the measure of *one* interior angle of a *regular* polygon. If you see one of these problems, here's what you do:

$$\frac{(n-2)180°}{n}$$

Remember that *n* stands for the number of sides (which is the same as the number of angles), so here's how to find a single angle measure of a regular pentagon:

$$\frac{(5-2)180°}{5} = \frac{(3)180°}{5} = \frac{540°}{5} = 108°$$

WARNING

PLAY

Be sure that the polygon is *regular* or *equiangular*. The question will typically state this, but if it doesn't, look for some other clue in the question to find the measure of that angle.

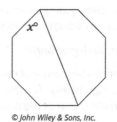

© John Wiley & Sons, Inc.

The preceding drawing shows a regular 8-sided polygon. What is the value of *x*?

(A) 52.5

(B) 55

(C) 62.5

(D) 65

(E) 67.5

The term *regular* means that all the sides and angles are the same. First, find the measure of one angle: Take the total of all the angles, and divide by the number of angles, which in this case is 8. The equation sums it all up:

$$\frac{(n-2)180°}{n}$$
$$\frac{((8)-2)180°}{(8)}$$
$$\frac{(6)180°}{8}$$
$$\frac{1080°}{8}$$
$$135°$$

Next, you know the segment bisects the angle because shape is regular, so divide this angle measure in half:

$$\frac{135°}{2} = 67.5°$$

So the answer is (E). See, even though the drawing is to scale, you can't just eyeball the answer. You have to know the rules and constructs of geometry.

Triangles

The *triangle* has three sides and is a key figure in GRE geometry. Understanding how triangles work helps you understand other polygons. The following sections introduce you to certain common triangles and explain how to do the related math.

Three common types of triangle are equilateral, isosceles, and right:

>> An *equilateral triangle* has three equal sides and three equal angles. Though technically it's also a *regular* or *equiangular triangle*, it's known as equilateral.

In the figure, the curved lines with the double lines through them inside the triangle tell you that the angles are equal. The short lines through the sides of the triangle tell you that the sides are equal.

>> An *isosceles triangle* has two equal sides and two equal angles. Note that any triangle that's *equilateral* (with three equal sides) is also *isosceles* (with two equal sides).

>> A *right* triangle has one 90-degree angle.

The little box in the bottom-left corner of the triangle tells you that the angle is 90 degrees. If the triangle *looks* like a right triangle but the question or drawing doesn't clearly state that it is (that is, with the box in the corner of the drawing), don't assume that it's a right triangle.

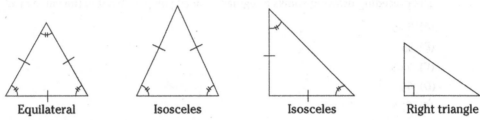

| Equilateral | Isosceles | Isosceles | Right triangle |

© John Wiley & Sons, Inc.

Measuring key characteristics

Triangles have some characteristics that help you field some questions on the exam. These may be intuitive, but study them just to be sure:

>> **The largest angle is opposite the longest side.** Conversely, the smallest angle is opposite the shortest side. (Remember that $\sqrt{3}$ is between 1 and 2.)

© John Wiley & Sons, Inc.

>> **The sum of any two side lengths is greater than any third side length.** This idea can be written as $a + b > c$, where *a*, *b*, and *c* are the sides of the triangle.

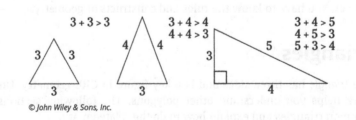

© John Wiley & Sons, Inc.

If two sides of a triangle have lengths 7 and 8, the length of the third side must be between

(A) 0 and 7

(B) 1 and 8

(C) 1 and 15

(D) 7 and 15

(E) 8 and 15

Start with 7 and 8 as *a* and *b*, and find the longest that the third side can be:

$$a+b>c$$
$$(7)+(8)>c$$
$$15>c$$

So the third side, *c* in this case, has to be less than 15. So what's the *shortest* that it can be? Use the same equation, this time with 7 and 8 as *a* and *c*:

$$a+b>c$$
$$(7)+b>(8)$$
$$b>1$$

The third side, *b* in this case, has to be greater than 1, which makes the answer (C).

Drawing perimeter and area

You may encounter at least one question that asks for the perimeter or area of a triangle. The following sections can help you clear that hurdle.

Perimeter is the distance around the triangle, so add up the lengths of the sides. This is true for any shape.

The area of a triangle is $\frac{base \times height}{2}$. This formula works *only* on a triangle. The height is a line perpendicular to the base. In a right triangle, the height is one of the sides. The height may be inside the triangle, represented by a dashed line and a 90-degree box.

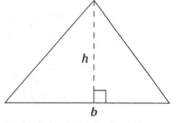

© John Wiley & Sons, Inc.

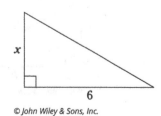

© John Wiley & Sons, Inc.

The area of the triangle is 12. What is the value of x?

Enter your answer:

_____

Did you automatically answer 2, as though the triangle were a rectangle? A rectangle's area is *length* times *width*, which in this case would be $2 \times 6 = 12$, covered further in "Quadilaterals." As a *triangle*, the area is $\frac{base \times height}{2}$, so place the numbers from the drawing, where x is the height:

$$a = \frac{base \times height}{2}$$
$$(12) = \frac{(6) \times height}{2}$$
$$24 = 6 \times height$$
$$4 = height$$

The answer is 4. Don't feel bad. I had an engineer miss this one.

An *equilateral* triangle has a specific formula for the area. $\frac{base \times height}{2}$ certainly works, but you need the height, and if the GRE doesn't give you the height, use $\frac{s^2\sqrt{3}}{4}$, where s is a side length.

Measuring with the Pythagorean theorem

The *Pythagorean theorem* works only on a right triangle. It states that the sum of the squares of the two shorter sides is equal to the square of the hypotenuse. If you know the lengths of any two sides, you can find the length of the third side, with this formula:

$$a^2 + b^2 = c^2$$

Here, a and b are the shorter sides of the triangle, and c is the hypotenuse. The hypotenuse is always opposite the 90-degree angle and the longest side of the triangle.

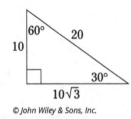

© John Wiley & Sons, Inc.

PLAY

Suppose that you're asked for the length of the base of this right triangle:

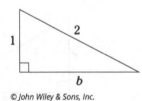

© John Wiley & Sons, Inc.

To find the unknown length of the third side, start with the Pythagorean theorem:

$$a^2 + b^2 = c^2$$

In this case, you know the a and the c, but you're missing the b. Place the side lengths that you have, and solve for the missing side:

$$a^2 + b^2 = c^2$$
$$(1)^2 + b^2 = (2)^2$$
$$1 + b^2 = 4$$
$$b^2 = 3$$
$$b = \sqrt{3}$$

REMEMBER

Before calculating the value of $\sqrt{3}$, check the answer choices. They will almost always be in terms of the radical. In this case, the calculator isn't your friend: If you're all set with the answer 1.732, and the answer choices are $\sqrt{2}$, $\sqrt{3}$, and $\sqrt{5}$, you'll have to start over.

TIP

You don't need the Pythagorean theorem for certain types of triangles if you know how to recognize them:

>> The two preceding triangles are examples of *common right triangles*. The sides of common right triangles reflect a ratio of 3:4:5 or 5:12:13. With a common right triangle, you don't need to work the Pythagorean theorem every time you need the third side length. For example if you know one side is 6 inches and another side is 8 inches, the 3:4:5 ratio tells you the third side is 10 inches.

>> Similarly, here's the ratio for the sides of an isosceles right triangle, also known as the 45-45-90 triangle (containing 45-45-90-degree angles), where s stands for side.

$$s : s : s\sqrt{2}$$

This ratio is also helpful when working with squares. If the side of a square is 5, and you need its diagonal, you know right away that said diagonal is $5\sqrt{2}$, because a square's diagonal cuts the square into two isosceles right triangles.

>> A 30-60-90 triangle (with angles measuring 30, 60, and 90 degrees) also has sides with a special ratio. Here's the ratio, where s is the length of the short side (opposite the 30-degree angle), $s\sqrt{3}$ is the longer side, and $2s$ is the hypotenuse.

$$s : s\sqrt{3} : 2s$$

PLAY

If the diagonal of a square is 5, what is the area of the square?

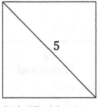

To find the area, first you need the length of a side. If the diagonal is 5, right away, you know the side length is $\frac{5}{\sqrt{2}}$, and the side-length ratio of the embedded 45-45-90 triangle is

$$\frac{5}{\sqrt{2}} : \frac{5}{\sqrt{2}} : 5$$

This means that each side of the square is $\frac{5}{\sqrt{2}}$. The area of any square is $a = s^2$ (discussed further in "Quadrilaterals"), making the area of this square

$$\left(\frac{5}{\sqrt{2}}\right)^2 = \frac{25}{2} = 12.5$$

Quadrilaterals

Any four-sided shape is a *quadrilateral*. The interior angles of any quadrilateral total 360 degrees, and you can cut any quadrilateral from corner to corner into two triangles. You know these shapes, but you need to know how they work mathematically, and more important, how they appear in GRE Math.

>> **Square:** The *square* has four equal sides and four right angles. The area of a square is length × width, but because *length* and *width* are the same, they're called *sides,* and the area is side^2.

>> **Rhombus:** A *rhombus* has four equal sides but angles that aren't right angles, like a square that got stepped on. It looks like a diamond, and its area is $\frac{1}{2}d_1d_2$, or $\left(\frac{1}{2}\text{diagonal}_1 \times \text{diagonal}_2\right)$. The rhombus isn't a common shape in GRE Math.

>> **Rectangle:** A *rectangle* has four right angles and opposite sides that are equal, and its area is length × width (which is the same as base × height).

>> **Parallelogram:** A *parallelogram* is like a rectangle with opposite sides that are equal, but the angles aren't necessarily right angles, like a rectangle that got stepped on. The area of a parallelogram is base × height, but the height is the distance between the two bases, not the length of one of the sides. The height is represented by a dotted line that's a right angle from one of the bases.

>> **Trapezoid:** A *trapezoid* has two sides that are parallel and two sides that are not parallel. The area of a trapezoid is like base × height, but because the bases have different lengths, you average them first captured by the clunky formula $\frac{\text{base}_1 + \text{base}_2}{2} \times \text{height}$. Just remember that it's simply base × height with the bases averaged.

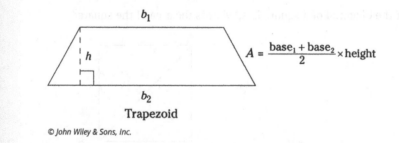

Trapezoid

© John Wiley & Sons, Inc.

>> **Other quadrilaterals:** Some quadrilaterals don't have specific shapes or names, but regardless, with 4 sides, the angles *always* total 360 degrees, the perimeter is *always* the distance around it, and if the question asks for the area, you can typically cut the shape into two triangles and measure those.

Circles

Determining a circle's *circumference* (distance around the circle) or area using its *radius* (the distance from the center of the circle to its edge) is simple with the formulas and features of the circle. The following sections take you back to school.

Identifying arts of a circle

The parts of a circle have specific names, and the GRE expects you to know these:

» **Center:** The *center* is the point in the middle of the circle. If a question refers to the circle by a capital letter, that's both the circle's center and its name.

» **Diameter:** The *diameter* is the width of the circle, often represented by a line segment that passes through the center and touches the opposite sides. The diameter is equal to twice the radius.

» **Circumference:** Known as a *perimeter* with other shapes, the *circumference* is the distance around the circle.

» **π, or *pi*:** Pronounced "pie," π is the ratio of the circumference to the diameter. It equals approximately 3.14, but circle-based questions usually have answer choices in terms of π, such as 2π, rather than 6.28.

» **Radius:** The *radius* is the distance from the center of the circle to the edge of the circle. The radius of a circle is half the diameter.

The radius is the same length regardless of which part of the edge of the circle it touches. This means that if a triangle is formed from two *radii* (the plural of radius) inside one circle, it's *always* isosceles and *could be* equilateral.

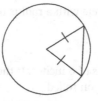

© John Wiley & Sons, Inc.

» **Tangent:** A *tangent* is a line outside a circle that touches the circle at one point.

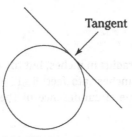

Tangent

© John Wiley & Sons, Inc.

» **Chord:** A *chord* is a line or segment that crosses through the circle and connects it on two points. The diameter is the circle's longest chord.

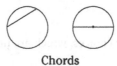

Chords

© John Wiley & Sons, Inc.

PLAY

Quantity A	Quantity B
Area of a circle of radius 6	Area of a circle with a longest chord of 12

(A) Quantity A is greater.

(B) Quantity B is greater.

(C) The two quantities are equal.

(D) The relationship cannot be determined from the information given.

The *longest chord* of a circle is the diameter. Because the diameter is twice the radius, a circle with diameter 12 has a radius of 6. In other words, the circles are the same size and have the same area. (Don't worry about solving for that area; you know the two circles are the same.) The correct answer is (C).

Calculating the circumference and area

You knew these equations, mastered them, and then forgot them. That's okay; they're right here.

The *circumference* is the distance around a circle, found with the equation $C = 2\pi r$ (where C is the circumference and r is radius). Because diameter is twice the radius, you may also use the equation $C = \pi d$ (where d is the diameter).

The circumference of a circle with a radius of 3 is

$$2\pi r = 2 \times \pi \times 3 = 6\pi$$

PLAY

A wagon has a wheel radius of 6 inches. If the wagon wheel travels 100 revolutions, approximately how many feet has the wagon rolled?

(A) 325

(B) 315

(C) 255

(D) 210

(E) 180

The question gives the radius in inches, but the answer choices are all in feet, so the first order of business is to convert inches into feet: $6 \div 12 = 0.5$ feet. One revolution of the wheel carries the wagon a distance of one circumference of the wheel, so find the circumference of the circle in feet:

$$C = 2\pi r$$
$$C = 2\pi (0.5)$$
$$C = \pi$$

Next, multiply by the number of revolutions:

$$\pi \times 100 = 100\pi \text{ feet}$$

Finally, check the answer choices, which are in real numbers, so replace π with 3.14 and multiply:

$$100 \times 3.14 = 314 \text{ feet}$$

Because the question reads *approximately*, go with 315 as an approximate of 314, so the correct answer is (B).

Area is the space inside the circle. The formula is $A = \pi r^2$, so if a circle has a radius of 4, you can find the area like this:

$$A = \pi(4)^2 = 16\pi$$

PLAY

What's the total approximate area, in square inches, of two 10-inch-diameter pizzas?

(A) 40

(B) 60

(C) 100

(D) 120

(E) 160

Only the GRE can make a math question out of a pizza. Actually, the SAT does this too. Anyway, the area equation takes the radius, but the question gives the diameter, so start by dividing the diameter in half for that radius: $10 \div 2 = 5$ inches.

Next, place that 5 in the area equation:

$$A = \pi r^2$$
$$A = \pi(5)^2$$
$$A = 25\pi$$

Check the answer choices, which are in real numbers, so replace π with 3.14 and multiply:

$$25 \times 3.14 = 78.5 \text{ inches}$$

Finally (and this is where the GRE trips testers up), the question asks about *two* pizzas, so take that answer and double it: $78.5 \times 2 = 157$. Because the question reads *approximately*, go with 160 as the closest approximate of 157. The correct answer is (E).

Measuring the arc

An *arc* is a part of the circumference of a circle and is typically formed by either a *central angle* or an *inscribed angle*:

» **Central angle:** A central angle has its vertex at the center of a circle and its endpoints on the circumference. The degree measure of a central angle is the same as the degree measure of its *minor arc* (the smaller arc).

» **Inscribed angle:** An inscribed angle has both its vertex and endpoints on the circumference. The degree measure of an inscribed angle is half the degree measure of its intercepted arc, as shown in the figure. The intercepted arc is 80 degrees, and the inscribed angle is half of that, at 40 degrees.

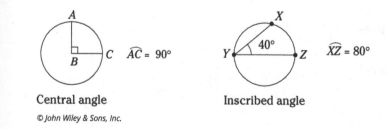

Central angle   Inscribed angle

With a *central* angle, the resulting arc has the *same* degree measure as the angle. With an *inscribed* angle, the resulting arc has *twice* the degree measure of the angle.

Even a drawing that looks like a dream-catcher, with lines all over, isn't so bad if you know how the vertices, arcs, and angles work.

In this figure, if minor arc $XY = 60°$, what is the sum of the degree measures of angles a, b, c, d, and e?

© John Wiley & Sons, Inc.

(A) 60

(B) 90

(C) 120

(D) 150

(E) 180

The angles a, b, c, d, and e are *inscribed angles*, meaning each angle has half the degree measure of its intercepted arc. You know from the drawing that the endpoints of each angle are X and Y, and the problem tells you that arc XY measures 60 degrees. This means that each angle is 30 degrees, for a total of $30 \times 5 = 150$. The correct answer is (D).

To find the length of an arc when you have its degree measure, follow these steps:

1. Find the circumference of the entire circle.

2. Put the degree measure of the arc over 360 and reduce the fraction.

3. Multiply the circumference by the fraction.

Find the length of minor arc AC:

© John Wiley & Sons, Inc.

(A) 36π

(B) 27π

(C) 18π

(D) 12π

(E) 6π

Take the steps one at a time:

1. **Find the circumference of the entire circle:**

$$C = 2\pi r$$
$$= 2\pi(18)$$
$$= 36\pi$$

Don't multiply π out; the answer choices are in terms of π.

2. **Put the degree measure of the arc over 360 and reduce the fraction.**

The degree measure of the arc is the same as its central angle, 60 degrees:

$$\frac{60}{360} = \frac{6}{36} = \frac{1}{6}$$

3. **Multiply the circumference by the fraction:**

$$36\pi \times \frac{1}{6} = 6\pi$$

The correct answer is (E).

WARNING

Be careful not to confuse the arc's *degree measure* with its *length*. The length is always part of the circumference and usually has a π in it. If you picked (E), you found the degree measure instead.

Shading the sector

A *sector* is part of the area of a circle that comes from a central angle. The degree measure of a sector is the same as the degree measure of that angle. On the GRE, you always see a sector from a *central* angle, never an *inscribed* angle.

To find the area of a sector, do the following:

1. **Find the area of the entire circle.**

2. **Put the degree measure of the sector over 360 and reduce the fraction.**

3. **Multiply the area by the fraction.**

Finding the area of a sector is similar to finding the length of an arc. The only difference is in the first step: You find the circle's *area*, not *circumference*. With this in mind, try a sample sector problem:

Find the area of minor sector *ABC*.

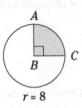

© John Wiley & Sons, Inc.

(A) 64π

(B) 36π

(C) 16π

(D) 12π

(E) 6π

Use the steps listed previously:

1. **Find the area of the entire circle.** $A = \pi r^2 = \pi (8)^2 = 64\pi$

2. **Put the degree measure of the sector over** $360°$**, and reduce the fraction.**

The sector is 90 degrees, same as its central angle:

$$\frac{90°}{360°} = \frac{1}{4}$$

3. **Multiply the area by the fraction:**

$$64\pi \times \frac{1}{4} = 16\pi$$

The correct answer is (C).

Finding the area of overlapping shapes

A question may present two shapes where one overlaps the other. The visible part of the shape underneath may be shaded, and the question typically asks you to calculate that shaded area. You don't always find an exact number, especially when one of the shapes is a circle.

PLAY

A circle of radius 4 inches is centered over an 8-inch square. Find the total shaded area.

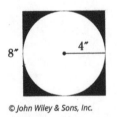

© John Wiley & Sons, Inc.

Here are two basic shapes where one overlaps the other. This is how to find that shaded part:

1. **Calculate the total area of the outside shape.**

Each side of the square is 8 inches:

$$8 \times 8 = 64$$

2. **Calculate the area of the inside shape.** $\pi r^2 = \pi (4)^2 = 16\pi$

3. **Subtract the area of the inside shape from the area of the outside shape.**

The difference between the two shapes is the shaded area. $64 - 16\pi$

And that's it! No calculating the exact number.

3D shapes

Three 3D shapes regularly appear on the GRE: the cylinder, the rectangular solid, and the cube. You typically find the *volume* of these shapes, and you may find the *surface area* of the cube. *Volume* refers to the space inside the shape (as in, how much water goes into a fish aquarium), and *surface area* refers to the area of the outside (as in, how much paper you would need to wrap a gift).

Calculating volume of a cylinder

The GRE calls its cylinders *right circular cylinders,* meaning that the top and bottom circles are the same size and perpendicular to the curved side, unlike, say, a cheerleading cone. Don't get caught up in it; it's basically a can of soup.

The volume of a cylinder is $V = \pi r^2 h$. Here's how you remember that: The base of the cylinder, as a circle, has an area of πr^2, times the height, h.

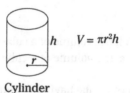

Cylinder

PLAY

What is the volume of a right circular cylinder having a radius of 3 and a height of 5?

(A) 15π

(B) 30π

(C) 45π

(D) 60π

(E) 75π

The volume of a cylinder is $V = \pi r^2 h$. Just place the radius and height, and find the volume:

$$V = \pi r^2 h$$
$$= \pi (3)^2 (5)$$
$$= 45\pi$$

The correct answer is (C).

Calculating volume of a rectangular solid

A rectangular solid on the GRE has six sides that are rectangles, basically like a shoebox. Multiply the lengths of the length, width, and height for the volume: $V = l \times w \times h$.

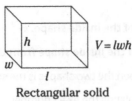

$V = lwh$

Rectangular solid

© John Wiley & S3ons, Inc.

PLAY

What is the volume of a rectangular shoebox having a length of 6, a width of 3, and a depth of 4?

(A) 72

(B) 60

(C) 48

(D) 36

(E) 24

Simple practice. Multiply out the dimensions for your answer:

$$V = 6 \times 3 \times 4 = 72.$$

The correct answer is (A).

Finding the volume of a cube

A *cube* is a rectangular solid where the dimensions are the same, like a six-sided *die* (one of a pair of dice). Because the *length*, *width*, and *height* are the same, they're called *edges* and represented by the letter *e*.

Like the rectangular solid, the volume of a cube is $V = l \times w \times h$. However, because the edges are the same and referred to as *e*, the volume of a cube is thus $V = e^3$.

PLAY

What is the edge length of a cube having volume of 1?

(A) $\frac{1}{3}$

(B) $\frac{1}{2}$

(C) 1

(D) 2

(E) 3

Don't get all cognitive on this one. Just go through the steps. You have the volume, so place that in the equation:

$$V = e^3$$
$$(1) = e^3$$
$$1 = e$$

The correct answer is (C). Trick question? Not for you.

Finding the surface area of a cube

The cube is typically the only shape where the GRE asks for the surface area. In fact, it'll give you the cube's volume, and you back-solve to find the surface area — or vice versa. Don't worry — it's just as doable as everything else in this chapter.

A cube has six identical faces, and each face is a square. The area of a square is $side^2$, or because each side is an *edge*, $edge^2$. And because the cube has six faces, the surface area is $6 \times edge^2$, or $6e^2$.

PLAY

If a cube has a volume of 8, what is its surface area?

(A) 8

(B) 12

(C) 16

(D) 24

(E) 32

First, back-solve the volume for the edge length:

$$V = e^3$$
$$8 = e^3$$
$$2 = e$$

And place that in the surface area equation:

$$SA = 6e^2$$
$$= 6(2)^2$$
$$= 24$$

The correct answer is (D).

Simplifying Word Problems

Most GRE Math is front and center, but sometimes you need to extract the math from a narrative in the form of a word problem. Fortunately, like all other GRE Math, you solve most word problems with one or more standard strategies. If you can recognize the type of problem and corresponding strategy, you'll do just fine. This section introduces common word problems along with those strategies for getting them right, fast.

Following the basic steps

When you're up against a word problem, knowing where to start is the key. Begin with the part that you know, and this will clarify the part that you don't know. You can solve almost all word problems with the following step-by-step approach:

1. **Check what kind of word problem it is.**

Word problems tend to be formula-heavy. If you recognize what kind of word problem it is, you automatically know which formula to use and thus how to solve it. That's what this section does for you.

2. **Write down the base formula.**

Most word problems are based on some formula, so write that down so you can fill in the blanks next. Sometimes you vary the formula based on your understanding of the word problem.

3. Place what you know into the formula.

The question provides info mixed into a story, and the formula gives you the framework to place the numbers as you *curate* (collect) the details. It also helps you stay organized. Just place what you know into the formula and solve for the rest.

TIP

When you write the equation from a sentence, remember that the word *is* becomes an equal sign. "Carly's age *is* twice David's age" becomes $c = 2d$. The same is true with variations of *is*, including *could be, would be,* and, of course, *was.*

When you have two unknowns, don't use both x and y if you can use x for both, especially when knowing one means you automatically know the other. For example, if Sally got some of 100 marbles and Alice got the rest, don't use s and a to represent the marbles given to Sally and Alice. Instead, use s and $100 - s$. The moment you know how many marbles Sally got, you automatically know how many went to Alice. If Sally got 40 marbles, you automatically know that Alice got 60.

4. Solve for what's missing.

Once you have everything in place, do the math. On the GRE, if you set the equation up properly, the math is *always* simple.

5. Make sure your answer fits the reality check.

If you have Grandma driving to LA at 200 miles per hour, check your work. Most word problems are in the context of a story, so you can reality-check to see whether the answer makes sense. My grandma got a speeding ticket — in a school zone. True story.

Setting up the formula for time and distance

No math set would be complete without two trains headed somewhere from Chattanooga. You'll probably encounter at least one question on the GRE that deals with distance, rate, and time. The question typically provides segments of a trip and asks for the average speed. To find this, place the total distance over the total time, and reduce the fraction to one hour (or whatever unit of time the question asks for). Solve it with this:

$$\frac{\text{total \# miles}}{\text{total \# hours}} = \frac{\text{miles (per hour)}}{1\,\text{hour}}$$

In its simplest form, if you drive 180 miles to Winslow in 3 hours, what was your average speed?

$$\frac{180\,\text{miles}}{3\,\text{hours}} = \frac{60\,\text{miles}}{1\,\text{hour}}$$

Your average speed was 60 miles per hour. On the trickier GRE-level questions, just total up the distance and place that over the total time. (You may have to convert minutes to hours.)

Jennifer drives 40 miles an hour for two and a half hours, and then 60 miles per hour for one and a half hours. What is her average speed?

PLAY

Finding Jennifer's total time is easier, so start with that: Per the story, she drove $2\frac{1}{2} + 1\frac{1}{2} = 4$ hours total. To find her total distance, work one part at a time. If she went 40 miles per hour for 2½ hours, then she went $40 \times 2\frac{1}{2} = 100$ miles for the first part, and 60 miles per hour for 1½ hours is $60 \times 1\frac{1}{2} = 90$ miles, for a total of $100 + 90 = 190$ miles. Set up the fraction and reduce it to 1 hour, like this:

$$\frac{190\,\text{miles}}{4\,\text{hours}} = \frac{47.5\,\text{miles}}{1\,\text{hour}}$$

Jennifer drove at an average speed of 47.5 miles per hour, which makes sense: You would expect the answer to fall between 40 and 60 miles per hour.

Simplifying units of measurement

In a conversion question, the GRE gives you the relationship between the units of measurement, *except* for units of time (for example, you won't be told that 60 seconds is 1 minute). If you're asked how many ounces are in 5 pounds, the question tells you that 1 pound is 16 ounces. To solve the problem, take the following steps:

1. Set up the conversion equations as fractions, with the terms (in this case, lbs) on opposite sides of the fraction.

$$\left(\frac{5 \text{ lb}}{1}\right)\left(\frac{16 \text{ oz}}{1 \text{ lb}}\right)$$

2. Cancel the common terms.

In this example, the *lb* units appear in the numerator and the denominator, so they cancel:

$$\left(\frac{5 \cancel{\text{ lb}}}{1}\right)\left(\frac{16 \text{ oz}}{1 \cancel{\text{ lb}}}\right)$$

3. Multiply the fractions.

$$\left(\frac{80 \text{ oz}}{1}\right) = 80 \text{ oz}$$

PLAY

If Murray runs at a constant rate of 15 kilometers per hour, how many meters does he run in two minutes? (1 kilometer = 1,000 meters)

(A) 200

(B) 500

(C) 8,000

(D) 16,000

(E) 18,000

First, find the meters he runs in *one* minute:

1. Set up the conversion equations as fractions, with the terms opposite.

$$\left(\frac{15 \text{ km}}{1 \text{ hour}}\right)\left(\frac{1,000 \text{ meters}}{1 \text{ km}}\right)\left(\frac{1 \text{ hour}}{60 \text{ minutes}}\right)$$

2. Cancel the common terms.

$$\left(\frac{15}{1}\right)\left(\frac{1,000 \text{ meters}}{1}\right)\left(\frac{1}{60 \text{ minutes}}\right)$$

3. Multiply the fractions.

$$\frac{15,000 \text{ meters}}{60 \text{ minutes}} = \frac{250 \text{ meters}}{1 \text{ minute}}$$

Now double your 250-meters-per-minute result for his two-minute distance of 500 meters and Choice (B).

Finding averages

You can always find the average in the way your teacher taught you in fifth grade: Add the terms together and divide by the number of terms. Say you want to find the average of 5, 11, 17, 23, and 29. First, add them all up:

$$5 + 11 + 17 + 23 + 29 = 85$$

Next, divide the total by the number of terms, which is 5:

$$\frac{85}{5} = 17$$

This method works every time, regardless of the numbers.

The following sections reveal shortcuts for tackling problems that are variations on this theme, including questions about missing-term averages and weighted averages.

Missing-term averages

For these types of questions, the GRE turns things around: It gives you the average and asks you for one of the missing terms. Say it tells you that the average is 10, and three of the numbers are 1, 8, and 13, so what's the missing number? You know what to do. Start with the formula:

$$\text{Average} = \frac{a + b + c + d}{4}$$

Place the numbers that you know into the formula, like this:

$$10 = \frac{1 + 8 + 13 + d}{4}$$

Then solve for d:

$$10 = \frac{22 + d}{4}$$
$$40 = 22 + d$$
$$d = 18$$

PLAY

A student takes seven exams. Her scores on the first six are 91, 89, 85, 92, 90, and 88. What score does she need on the *seventh* exam for an average of 90 to get an A?

Set up the formula with x as the seventh exam score:

$$90 = \frac{91 + 89 + 85 + 92 + 90 + 88 + x}{7}$$

Then solve for x by adding the numbers and multiplying by 7:

$$90 = \frac{535 + x}{7}$$
$$630 = 535 + x$$
$$x = 95$$

The student's seventh exam score needs to be 95 for that A. They'll get it.

Evenly spaced integers

You can quickly find the average when the integers are evenly spaced, including consecutive. *Consecutive* means that the numbers come one right after another, as in {2, 3, 4, 5}. *Evenly spaced* means that the terms are the same distance apart, as in {5, 10, 15, 20}. Whether the terms are consecutive or evenly spaced, use one of these methods to find the average:

>> If the number of terms is odd, the average is equal to the middle term. For example, {3, 4, 5, 6, 7} has an average of 5.

>> If the number of terms is even, the average is equal to the average of the two middle terms. For example, {10, 12, 14, 16} has an average of 13 because $\frac{12+14}{2} = \frac{26}{2} = 13$.

>> Regardless of the number of terms, when the terms are evenly spaced, the average is always the average of the first and the last terms. For example, {22, 26, 30, 34, 38} has an average of 32 because $\frac{22+38}{2} = \frac{60}{2} = 30$ (and the middle number is 30).

PLAY

Find the average of these evenly spaced numbers:

{50, 59, 68, 77, 86}

Don't reach for your pencil. Instead, use the fact that the terms are evenly spaced. Because the set contains an odd number of terms, go for the middle number: The average is 68. You could also average the first and last numbers: $\frac{50+86}{2} = 68$. Either way is less work than averaging *all* the numbers.

Weighted averages

A *weighted average* is the average of groups, where you have the average value for each group. For example, five juniors have an average score of 120, and ten seniors have an average score of 90. The larger the group, the more it affects — weights — the total average. The ten seniors affect the total average more than the five juniors do because the group of seniors is larger, regardless of the test scores.

TIP

If the larger group has a greater effect on the average, then the average is always closer to the larger group. With the preceding example, there are more seniors than juniors, so you know right away — without doing *any* math — that the students' total average score is closer to the seniors' average of 90 than to the juniors' average of 120.

To calculate a weighted average, multiply each value (each specific score) by the number in the group (the number of students who got that score). Do this for each group, add the products together, and divide this sum by the total number in all the groups (here, the total number of students).

PLAY

Find the weighted average score for 15 students with the following scores:

Number of Students	Score
5	120
10	90

Because 5 students got a 120, multiply $5 \times 120 = 600$. Do the same with the other score: $10 \times 90 = 900$. Now add them up:

$600 + 900 = 1,500$

You now have the total number of points that all the students earned. To find the total average, divide the 1,500 by the total number of students, which is $5 + 10 = 15$:

$$\frac{1,500}{15} = 100$$

The average score is 100.

TIP

It's good to know how to calculate the weighted average, but you won't have to do this very often. It's more common that you're tested on how well you *understand* it — specifically, that the total average is closer to the larger group.

Handling work problems

Work problems typically tell you how long individuals take to complete a task working alone and then ask you how long they'd take to complete the task working together. To solve a work problem, use this formula:

$$\frac{1}{\text{Time}_A} + \frac{1}{\text{Time}_B} = \frac{1}{\text{Time}_{\text{Total}}}$$

where Time_A is the time it takes the first person (A), Time_B is the time it takes the second person (B), and so on. This formula works with as many people as could be in a GRE question. $\text{Time}_{\text{Total}}$ is the total time it takes all of them working together. If you have more than two people working, just put 1 over the time each one takes and add that to the total.

PLAY

If Natasha can paint a house in six days and David can paint the same house in eight days, how many days does it take them, working together, to paint the house?

To solve this problem, place the numbers and do the math:

$$\frac{1}{\text{Time}_A} + \frac{1}{\text{Time}_B} = \frac{1}{\text{Time}_{\text{Total}}}$$

$$\left(\frac{1}{6}\right) + \left(\frac{1}{8}\right) = \frac{1}{\text{Time}_{\text{Total}}}$$

$$\frac{8}{48} + \frac{6}{48} =$$

$$\frac{14}{48} =$$

$$\frac{7}{24} =$$

Then reciprocate the fractions and simplify:

$$\frac{7}{24} = \frac{1}{\text{Time}_{\text{Total}}}$$

$$\frac{24}{7} = \text{Time}_{\text{Total}}$$

$$3\frac{3}{7} = \text{Time}_{\text{Total}}$$

Working together, Natasha and David would take $3\frac{3}{7}$ days to paint the house.

WARNING

Be sure to reality-check your answer. If you get an answer of ten days, for example, you know there's a mistake because the two of them working *together* should take *less* time than either one working alone.

Figuring out team-work problems

A *team-work problem* gives you a team of workers (or machines) where each works at the same rate, and the problem tells you that the team accomplishes a certain task in a certain amount of time. For example, 12 factory workers accomplish a certain task in 10 days. Then the problem asks for either the new number of days required with a different number of workers or the new number of workers required with a different number of days. Either way, you solve it exactly the same way, with this formula:

(old # workers)(old # days) = (new # workers)(new # days)

PLAY

If 12 workers can accomplish a certain task in 10 days, how many days are needed to accomplish the same task with only 8 workers?

Use the formula, with x as the new number of days:

$$(\text{old \# workers})(\text{old \# days}) = (\text{new \# workers})(\text{new \# days})$$
$$(12)(10) = (8)(x)$$
$$120 = 8x$$
$$x = 15$$

8 workers would require 15 days to accomplish the same task.

REMEMBER

Besides describing machines instead of workers, the problem may describe hours instead of days. Solve it exactly the same way, and don't worry about converting.

Instead of saying, "to do a certain task," the problem may read, "to produce 240 drones." If that number doesn't change, don't worry about it; if that number *does* change, apply the ratio of the change to your answer. For example, if the factory now needs 480 drones, which is twice the original 240, then double your answer.

TIP

Simplifying mixture problems

A mixture problem looks more confusing than it actually is. The key to solving it is to set up a table that accounts for both the total mix and the component parts, as in the following example.

PLAY

Carolyn wants to mix 40 pounds of almonds selling for 30 cents a pound with x pounds of dark chocolate selling for 80 cents a pound. She wants to pay 40 cents per pound for the final mix. How many pounds of dark chocolate should she use?

The hardest part for most test-takers is knowing where to begin. Begin with these steps:

1. **Make a table and start with the labels for all the data you have.**

	Pounds	Price	Total
Almonds			
Dark Chocolate			
Mixture			

2. **Fill in the values that the test question gives you.**

Almonds are 40 pounds at 30 cents a pound, and dark chocolate is 80 cents per pound. Carolyn wants the mixture to cost 40 cents a pound.

	Pounds	Price	Total
Almonds	40	$0.30	
Dark Chocolate		$0.80	
Mixture		$0.40	

3. **Use *x* for your unknown value.**

If Carolyn starts with 40 pounds of almonds and adds *x* pounds of dark chocolate, she ends up with $40 + x$ pounds of mixture.

	Pounds	Price	Total
Almonds	40	$0.30	
Dark Chocolate	x	$0.80	
Mixture	$40 + x$	$0.40	

4. **Multiply across the rows to fill in the Total column.**

The total cost of almonds is $40 \times \$0.30 = \$12.00$, the total cost of dark chocolate is $0.80 times *x*, and the total cost of the whole mixture is $0.40 times the total weight, which is $(40 + x)$.

	Pounds	Price	Total
Almonds	40	$0.30	$12.00
Dark Chocolate	x	$0.80	$0.80x
Mixture	$40 + x$	$0.40	$0.40(40+x)

5. **Solve for *x*.**

In the Total column, the total cost of almonds plus the total cost of dark chocolate equals the total cost of the mixture, so the equation looks like this:

$$\$12.00 + \$0.80x = \$0.40(40 + x)$$

Next, distribute the $0.40 on the right, and it all falls into place:

$$\$12.00 + \$0.80x = \$16.00 + \$0.40x$$
$$\$0.40x = \$4.00$$
$$x = 10$$

Keep in mind that *x* stands for the number of pounds of dark chocolate, which is what the question asks for. See, that's the point of GRE word problems: Set up the formula, place what you know, and solve for the missing part.

Finding answers about sets and groups

Sets and *groups* are problems that place numbers, objects, or any items whatsoever into groups and describe the relationships between those groups. For example, you may group students by juniors and seniors and have members of each group form a subset for athletes. The following sections show you what the GRE may ask and how to answer it.

REMEMBER

A *set* is a collection of numbers, values, or objects that are typically related in some way, like this: {1, 3, 5, 7, 9}.

The Venn diagram

Some members of one set also belong to another set, and vice versa, creating an overlap. For example, some students in history class are also in physics class, and the *intersection* is the students taking both classes, shown by the upside-down *u*-shaped symbol: ∩. The right-side-up *u*-shaped symbol indicates a *union*, which is *all* the students: ∪.

> » **Union:** The union of the sets A and B, using the symbol $A \cup B$, contains *all* the members of both sets. If Set $A = \{2, 3, 5\}$ and Set $B = \{3, 5, 7\}$, then $A \cup B = \{2, 3, 5, 7\}$.
>
> » **Intersection:** The intersection of the sets A and B, using the symbol $A \cap B$, contains *only* members belonging to both sets. If Set $A = \{2, 3, 5\}$ and Set $B = \{3, 5, 7\}$, then $A \cap B = \{3, 5\}$.

A *Venn diagram* shows the relationship between sets, including the union and intersection. It always has two or three circles representing sets, and these circles overlap to show the relationships between members of the sets. If the problem describes two groups with some members in both groups, draw a Venn diagram to visualize it.

PLAY

What is in the intersection of sets A and B?

   A = {cars, trucks, boats, vans}

   B = {boats, vans, ATVs, motorcycles}

(A) cars, trucks

(B) nothing

(C) cars, trucks, boats, vans, ATVs, motorcycles

(D) boats, vans

(E) A, B

The *intersection* of A and B has only the members that are in both sets. Only boats and vans are in both groups. The correct answer is Choice (D). If you picked Choice (C), you went with union instead of intersection.

The sets formula

A Venn diagram is effective to count small numbers or to sort specific members within the groups. When the problem has you work with larger numbers in the groups, use the sets formula:

$$(\# \text{ in set } 1) + (\# \text{ in set } 2) - (\cap \text{ sets } 1 \text{ and } 2) = \text{total } \#$$

PLAY

Ninety students are taking either history, physics, or both. If 65 are taking history and 45 are taking physics, how many students are in both classes?

As always, start with the formula, place the numbers that you know, and solve for what's missing:

$$(\# \text{ in set } 1) + (\# \text{ in set } 2) - (\cap \text{ sets } 1 \text{ and } 2) = \text{total } \#$$
$$(65) + (45) - x = (90)$$
$$110 - x = 90$$
$$x = 20$$

Determining probability

A *probability* question may ask your chances of throwing a pair of dice and getting a total of seven or snake eyes (1s on both dice). Fortunately, three simple steps can help you solve nearly every probability problem thrown your way, both in general and with multiple events. I also show you how to handle a probability problem involving sets and groups.

REMEMBER

A probability is always a number between 0 and 1. A probability of 0 means that the event *won't* happen, and a probability of 1, or 100 percent, means it *will* happen. The probability that something *will* happen plus the probability that something *won't* happen always equals 1. A probability can't be negative or greater than 1.

Step #1: Set up the fraction

To find a probability, start with this formula to create a fraction:

$$\text{Probability} = \frac{\text{Number of desired outcomes}}{\text{Number of total outcomes}}$$

First, find the denominator, which is the total number of outcomes. For example, when you're rolling a six-sided die, there are six possible outcomes, giving you a denominator of 6. When you're pulling a card out of a standard deck, there are 52 possible outcomes (because a full deck has 52 cards), giving you a denominator of 52.

Next, find the numerator, which shows the total number of things you want. If you want to get a 5 when you roll a die, a die has exactly one 5 on it, so the numerator is 1. The probability of rolling a 5 is $\frac{1}{6}$. What's the probability of drawing a jack out of a standard deck of cards? The deck has 52 cards (the denominator) and 4 jacks (the numerator), so the probability is $\frac{4}{52}$, which reduces to $\frac{1}{13}$. The probability of drawing the jack of hearts, however, is only $\frac{1}{52}$ because a standard deck of cards contains only one jack of hearts.

PLAY

A jar of marbles has 8 yellow marbles, 6 black marbles, and 12 white marbles. What is the probability of drawing out a black marble?

With 26 marbles total and 6 black marbles, the probability is $\frac{6}{26}$, or $\frac{3}{13}$.

Step #2: Multiply consecutive probabilities

A *consecutive probability* is just a fancy term for events that happen more than once and don't affect each other (meaning they're *independent*). For example, if you flip a coin twice, the probability that it lands heads both times is a consecutive probability because the outcome of the first toss has no bearing on the outcome of the second toss. To find the probability of a specific set of events — that is, landing heads on both tosses — find the separate probability of each event and then multiply them.

The probability of landing heads is $\frac{1}{2}$ for the first toss and $\frac{1}{2}$ for the second, so multiply these together:

$$\frac{1}{2} \times \frac{1}{2} = \frac{1}{4}$$

The probability of getting heads twice on two tosses is 1 out of 4.

Step #3: Add either/or probabilities on a single event

An *either/or probability* on a single event is one in which either of two outcomes is desired. For example, if you reach into a bag containing 10 blue, 10 red, and 10 green marbles, what's the probability that you draw either a blue marble *or* a red marble? To solve this problem, find the probability of each event separately and then add them together. With 10 red marbles in a bag of 30, drawing a red marble has a 1 in 3 chance of occurring; drawing a blue marble is also 1 in 3:

$$\frac{1}{3} \text{ and } \frac{1}{3}$$

Add these together for the probability of drawing either a blue or a red marble:

$$\frac{1}{3} + \frac{1}{3} = \frac{2}{3}$$

You could also add the red and blue marbles first. To draw one of 10 blue marbles or 10 red marbles, there are 20 marbles total that would work, out of 30 marbles total in the bag, for the same answer:

$$\frac{20}{30} = \frac{2}{3}$$

Simplifying probability in sets and groups

Sets and groups and probability (discussed in the previous sections) can be packaged into a single GRE question. Apply what you've already learned to answer these questions:

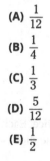

PLAY

Of the 12 applicants for a job, 6 have master's degrees, 5 have tenure, and 4 have neither the degree nor the tenure. If one applicant is called at random, what is the probability that they have both a master's degree and tenure?

(A) $\frac{1}{12}$

(B) $\frac{1}{4}$

(C) $\frac{1}{3}$

(D) $\frac{5}{12}$

(E) $\frac{1}{2}$

Start with the probability fraction:

$$\text{Probability} = \frac{\text{Number of desired outcomes}}{\text{Number of total outcomes}}$$

The number of total possible outcomes is easy: 12 candidates, so 12 is the denominator. The challenge is finding the number of possible desired outcomes. Because this example has members who are in neither group (having neither a master's degree nor tenure), use the sets formula, but add a third group for neither:

$$\text{Group}_1 + \text{Group}_2 + \text{Neither} - \text{Both} = \text{Total}$$
$$\text{Master's} + \text{Tenure} + \text{Neither} - \text{Both} = \text{Total}$$
$$(6) + (5) + (4) - x = 12$$
$$15 - x = 12$$
$$x = 3$$

Three applicants have both a master's degree and tenure. Place the 3 over the total number of applicants, 12:

$$\frac{3}{12} = \frac{1}{4}$$

The correct answer is Choice (B).

Simplifying counting methods

Counting certainly sounds easy enough, but when you're counting the number of ways different things can be arranged, counting becomes less intuitive. The following sections explain some methods to make complex counting intuitive again.

Basic counting methods

Suppose you have five shirts, two pairs of pants, and two jackets. How many different outfits can you put together? To answer this question, follow these steps:

1. **Make a space for each item that can change.**

   In this case, you have three spaces: one each for shirts, pants, and jackets.

2. **In each space, write down the number of options.**

   You now have something like this:

Shirts	Pants	Jackets
5	2	2

3. **Multiply the numbers.**

   $5 \times 2 \times 2 = 20$ different outfits.

This is how you count the possible combinations when rolling two six-sided dice. Each die has six possible outcomes, so the total number of different ways the numbers on the dice can be combined is $6 \times 6 = 36$.

PLAY

A gelato shop has ten no-sugar-added flavors, three types of cones, and two toppings. If your date gets one no-sugar-added flavor on a cone with one topping, how many possibilities are there?

(A) 60

(B) 50

(C) 40

(D) 30

(E) 20

Make a space for each item that can change. With ten flavors, three cones, and two toppings, your drawing looks like this:

$$\underline{10} \times \underline{3} \times \underline{2}$$

Serve up your answer:

$$\underline{10} \times \underline{3} \times \underline{2} = 60$$

The answer is a low-carb Choice (A).

When order matters: Permutations

A *permutation* is a change in the arrangement of a given number of items or events. If the order in which items are arranged matters, you're looking at a permutation problem. One of the simplest examples looks at the possible number of ways the letters A, B, and C can be arranged (the possible number of permutations). The answer is six:

ABC   BAC   CAB

ACB   BCA   CBA

Based on the counting method discussed in the preceding section, you can figure this out without having to write out each possible permutation. The first event (or letter in this case) has three possible outcomes (A, B, or C), the second event has two possible outcomes (the remaining two letters), and the third event has only one possible outcome (the last remaining letter):

1st Letter	2nd Letter	3rd Letter
3	2	1

Multiplying gives you $3 \times 2 \times 1 = 6$

When a question asks for the possible number of ways a certain number of objects may be arranged or events may occur, you can also use the factorial. (See "Factorials" earlier in this block.) The *factorial* is indicated by an exclamation point (!) and represents the product of integers up to and including a specific integer, so 3!, which stands for "three factorial," is $3 \times 2 \times 1 = 6$.

You can solve simple permutation problems using $n!$, where n represents the number of objects to arrange or the order of events.

PLAY

Toby, Jill, Ashley, and Mark are racing bicycles. If there are no ties, in how many different orders can they finish the race?

Because there are four racers, the number of different orders in which they can finish is $4! = 4 \times 3 \times 2 \times 1 = 24$.

A permutation problem may ask about a small part of a larger group, such as the number of ways in which three kids out of a class of ten can be seated in the front row, or the number of ways in which three runners out of ten can place first, second, and third. Basically, if the order matters, it's a permutation problem.

Although there are two methods to solve this, the following method uses a formula that leads to a better understanding of *combinations*, covered in the next section. The formula uses the factorial:

$$P_r^n = \frac{n!}{(n-r)!}$$

Where P is the number of permutations you're trying to determine, n is the total number of objects or events, and r is the subset of objects or events you're working with. (Note that near the P, the 10 below, and the n above, are not *exponents*: They're *indicators*.) In this example, $n = 10$ and $r = 3$. Place the numbers and do the math:

$$P_3^{10} = \frac{10!}{(10-3)!} = \frac{10!}{7!}$$

The numbers will always be simple and easy to multiply. You can make the calculations easier by reducing the fraction to its simplest terms first and then multiplying the remaining factors in the factorial:

$$P_3^{10} = \frac{10 \times 9 \times 8 \times 7!}{7!} = 720$$

PLAY

Nate is expecting eight families, each in a separate car, to attend the picnic. If there are only two parking spaces in front, and each space holds one car, how many ways can two cars park in front?

Because order matters, this is a permutation problem. In this example, you have eight total cars, but you're working with only two of those cars, so $n = 8$ and $r = 2$. Place the numbers and do the math:

$$P_2^8 = \frac{8!}{(8-2)!} = \frac{8!}{6!}$$

Reduce the fraction to its simplest terms and then multiply the remaining numbers:

$$P_2^8 = \frac{8 \times 7 \times 6!}{6!}$$
$$= 8 \times 7$$
$$= 56$$

When order doesn't matter: Combinations

A *combination* is a subset of objects or events in which order doesn't matter (for example, choosing 4 different business cards from a bowl containing 20 different cards). If a question asks about choosing a number of items and the order in which items are arranged or events occur doesn't matter, it's a combination problem. Use this formula:

$$C_r^n = \frac{n!}{r!(n-r)!}$$

where C is the number of combinations you're trying to determine, n is the total number of objects or events, and r is the number of objects or events you're choosing. (As with the Permutations formula, the n near the C is not an *exponent*: It's an *indicator*.)

PLAY

From a group of ten colleagues, Sally must choose three to serve on a committee. How many possible combinations does she have to choose from?

Because the order doesn't matter, this is a combination problem, so proceed as follows:

$$C_3^{10} = \frac{10!}{3!(10-3)!}$$
$$= \frac{(10)(\cancel{9}^3)(\cancel{8}^4)(\cancel{7!})}{(\cancel{3}^1)(\cancel{2}^1)(1)(\cancel{7!})}$$
$$= 120$$

Interpreting Data and Graphs

Regardless of your area of study or your choice of grad school, you need a general understanding of how tables and graphs describe statistics and data. The folks who developed the GRE are well aware of this, so they include several questions in the math sections of the exam to test your skills in data analysis. This section gets you up to speed on interpreting graphs and data as they appear in the GRE.

Interpreting Basic Stats

With a few concepts, you can solve pretty much any basic statistics problem on the GRE. In this section, I cover the concepts of median, mode, range, mean, and standard deviation.

Median

The *median* is the middle number when all the terms are arranged in order. Think of the median strip in the middle of a road. To find the median, place the numbers in order.

If the list has an even number of terms, put them in order and find the middle two, and take the average of those two terms.

PLAY

Find the median of 5, 0, −3, −5, 1, 2, 8, 6.

(A) 0

(B) 1

(C) 1.5

(D) 2

(E) 5

Put the numbers in order: −5, −3, 0, 1, 2, 5, 6, 8. The middle two terms are 1 and 2, and their average is 1.5. That's it. Correct answer: Choice (C).

Mode

The *mode* is the most frequent number. Think *mode* rhymes (almost) with *most*. Put the numbers in order so you can more easily spot the number that shows up the most often — that's the mode.

PLAY

Find the modes of 6, 7, 8, 8, 8, 9, 10, 10, 11, 11, 11, 12, 15. Select *all* answers that apply.

(A) 6

(B) 8

(C) 10

(D) 11

(E) 12

(F) 15

A group of numbers can have more than one mode. In this case, the group of numbers contains three 8s and three 11s, so it has two modes. Correct answers: Choices (B) and (D).

Range

The *range* is the distance from the smallest value to the largest value. You find the range by subtracting the smallest term from the largest term.

PLAY

If the range of the numbers 30, 40, 50, 70, 90, and x is 70, which of the following *could* be the value of x? Select <u>two</u> answers.

(A) 10

(B) 20

(C) 50

(D) 70

(E) 90

(F) 100

The range is the difference between the lowest and highest numbers. The lowest and highest numbers that you're given are 30 and 90, which have a difference of 60, so x has to be outside those numbers — either less than 30 or greater than 60. For a range of 70, x could be 20, because $90 - (20) = 70$, or it could be 100, because $(100) - 30 = 70$. The correct answers are Choices (B) and (F).

This is a common type of GRE range question.

Mean

Mean is another word for *average* (touched upon in "Finding averages" earlier in this block). You can review the earlier explanation and try the following practice question to see how this concept is also relevant to statistics.

PLAY

$x + y + z = 5$

Quantity A	Quantity B
The average of $(x + 4y - z)$, $(x + 2y + 2z)$, and $(x - 3y + 2z + 9)$	8

(A) Quantity A is greater.

(B) Quantity B is greater.

(C) The two quantities are equal.

(D) The relationship cannot be determined from the information given.

How do you find the average of three expressions? Add them up and divide by 3. Even though these aren't exactly numbers, it works the same way. First, set it up:

$$A = \frac{(x+4y-z)+(x+2y+2z)+(x-3y+2z+9)}{3}$$

Now drop the parentheses:

$$A = \frac{x+4y-z+x+2y+2z+x-3y+2z+9}{3}$$

I know it looks like madness. Remember how GRE Math works: If you set it up correctly, everything cancels out. Organize the madness by grouping the x's, y's, and z's:

$$A = \frac{x+x+x+4y+2y-3y-z+2z+2z+9}{3}$$
$$= \frac{3x+3y+3z+9}{3}$$

The question tells you that $x+y+z=5$, so $3x+3y+3z=15$. Plug that in and wrap this up:

$$A = \frac{15+9}{3}$$
$$= \frac{24}{3}$$
$$= 8$$

And that's the point: Don't be chilled by these crazy-looking equations. As long as you set them up correctly and don't drop a negative sign or make a silly mistake, you should have no problem solving them. The two quantities are equal, so the correct answer is Choice (C).

Standard deviation

Standard deviation for a set of numbers is a measure of the distance of each number from the mean. Standard deviation can be complicated, but on the GRE, it's always simple.

Every set of numbers has a mean, and each number in that set is either on the mean or a distance from it. For example, with the numbers 3, 5, 7, 9, and 11, the mean is 7, and the other numbers are either 2 or 4 from the mean.

Through a complex calculation (which you don't need to worry about), the distances of these points from the mean are mixed together to find the standard deviation. Though you don't need to know how to calculate standard deviation, you do need to know what it is.

If a set of data has a mean of 100 and a standard deviation of 10, then anything 10 away from the mean, whether above or below, is *within* that standard deviation. For example, 95, being less than 10 away from the mean of 100, is within the standard deviation, and 115, being more than 10 away from the mean, is outside the standard deviation.

PLAY

Members of the June High football team have an average height of 6 feet, 3 inches, with a standard deviation of 2.5 inches. Which of the following players are within the standard deviation? Select *all* correct answers.

(A) Smith: 5 feet, 10 inches

(B) Barnes: 6 feet, 1 inch

(C) Carly: 6 feet, 3 inches

(D) Henry: 6 feet, 2 inches

(E) Edwin: 5 feet, 11 inches

(F) Astor: 6 feet

Within one standard deviation is between 6 feet, 0.5 inches (2.5 inches below the mean), and 6 feet, 5.5 inches (2.5 inches above the mean). Barnes, Carly, and Henry are within these heights. Correct answers: Choices (B), (C), and (D).

TIP

A question may ask you to compare two or more standard deviations of a graph or a data set. Eyeballing them typically does the trick: If the data is generally farther from the mean, it has a greater standard deviation; if it's generally closer to the mean, it has a lesser standard deviation.

Distribution curve

The GRE expects you to understand the significance of the standard deviation. You don't have to calculate anything with this graph, but you do have to understand the normal distribution of data.

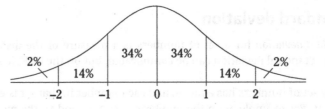

» Everything between –1 and 1 is within *one* standard deviation. With normal distribution, this is about 68% of the data.

» Everything between –2 and 2 is within *two* standard deviations and is about 95% of normal data.

» Everything between –3 and 3 is within *three* standard deviations and is just above 99% of normal data.

Interpreting tables and graphs

Among the math questions, the GRE presents a set of one or two tables and graphs along with about three questions based on that set of data — though there may also be a solo table/graph question here or there.

A *table* displays data in rows and columns, as in a channel guide or scoreboard. On the GRE, however, tables do more than help you find the game or the score: They contain details for analyzing the data.

A *graph*, discussed in the next section, is a drawing that visually shows the relationship between the data and how the data changes. The graphs are always drawn to scale, so you can rely on them as accurate visual representations of the data. To alleviate any doubt, the graphs typically include a note that says, "Graphs drawn to scale."

TIP

The grouped table and graph questions aren't more challenging than the other math questions, but do take more time. A good time-management strategy is to guess on the table/graph questions, mark them for review as explained in Block 1, and return to them when you've finished the other questions.

REMEMBER

To handle the table and graph questions, you need an eye for detail and a knack for understanding what the data tells you. In other words, the GRE challenges you to determine the significance of the data. Take the following approach to answering any question that contains a table:

1. Look over the data for a sense of what it's describing.

2. Check for details, such as numbers versus percents, and if the data is over time, whether it's in days, months, or years.

3. Carefully read the question and understand *exactly* what it's asking.

4. Look at the answer choices: If they're far apart, you can estimate the answer.

5. From the table, find the details of what the question is asking.

6. Do your math and select the closest answer.

Following is an example of a question based on a table.

PLAY

Distribution of Television Shows Streamed by Category for 2021 and 2022

Category	2021	2022
Action	15.2%	13.7%
Comedy	18.9%	19.1%
Drama	7.4%	10.5%
Family	22.0%	19.2%
Foreign	4.8%	7.2%
Independent	5.6%	9.3%
Romance	8.1%	5.2%
Sci-Fi	5.3%	4.0%
Thriller	12.7%	11.8%
Total	100.0%	100.0%
Total shows streamed	3,225	4,189

Based on the information in the table, which of the following statements can you infer? Select *all* that are true.

(A) In each of the years 2021 and 2022, TV shows streamed in the Action, Drama, and Thriller categories accounted for more than 35 percent of all TV shows streamed.

(B) The total number of Sci–Fi shows streamed increased from 2021 to 2022.

(C) From 2021 to 2022, the total number of shows streamed increased by more than 25 percent.

Check each answer choice separately:

➤ For Choice (A), add the percentages in the Action, Drama, and Thriller categories for each year: $15.2 + 7.4 + 12.7 = 35.3\%$ and $13.7 + 10.5 + 11.8 = 36\%$, so Choice (A) is true.

➤ For Choice (B), multiply the Sci-Fi percentage by the total number of shows streamed for each year and compare the numbers: $0.053 \times 3,225 = 171$ for 2021 and $0.04 \times 4,189 = 168$ for 2022, so Choice (B) is false — the number of Sci-Fi shows streamed actually decreased slightly.

➤ For Choice (C), subtract 2021's total shows streamed from 2022's total shows streamed to determine how many more shows were streamed in 2022, and then divide by 2021's total shows streamed: $(4,189 - 3,225) \div 3,225 \times 100\% = 29\%$ (using the percent of change method from Chapter 10), so Choice (C) is true.

The correct answers are Choices (A) and (C).

Different types of graphs

To make sense of data presented in a graph, familiarize yourself with the following graph types (and if you're not sure what they look like, a quick internet search will provide examples):

➤ A *line graph* consists of two or three axes with data points connected by a line, sort of like a connect-the-dots exercise. How data points are plotted on the graph depends on the graph type:

   • **Two axes:** A typical line graph consists of an *x*- (horizontal) and *y*- (vertical) axis, each of which represents a different unit of measure.

   • **Three axes:** A graph with three axes contains a *y*-axis on the left and the right. You read the points on a three-axis graph the same way you do on a two-axis graph; just make sure you're clear on which *y*-axis each line refers to.

➤ A *bar graph,* also called a *column graph,* has vertical or horizontal bars that may represent actual numbers or percentages. Although they look significantly different from line graphs, they're very similar. The only difference is that the data points create bars instead of connecting to form a line.

➤ The *Gantt chart* is familiar to anyone who has worked as a project manager. Named for its inventor, Henry Gantt, the Gantt chart is a type of bar graph that tracks a timeline and shows the *sequence* and *dependency of events,* meaning one event has to conclude before the next one can begin. For example, you have to board the plane *before* you can fly to Hawaii. Your flight to Hawaii is *dependent* on you boarding that plane.

➤ Each *pie chart* represents 100 percent of the whole, while portions of the graph represent parts of that circle or slices of that pie. To read such a graph, first make a mental note of what the whole circle or pie represents so you know what each portion represents.

» A *logarithmic graph* is a graph with an axis scale that changes by multiples of 10. The axis isn't labeled with consecutive numbers (1, 2, 3, 4) or an evenly spaced pattern (5, 10, 15, 20). Instead, each increment is equal to the previous increment multiplied by 10 (1, 10, 100, 1,000, and so on). This graph is useful for tracking small changes with small numbers but ignoring small changes with large numbers.

» A *scatter plot* is useful for spotting trends and making predictions. It's similar to a line graph, but instead of connecting the individual dots, you draw a line to show the flow of data and predict where the future data points are likely to fall. This line is called a *trend line* or *regression line*. Sometimes the trend line is drawn, and other times you estimate it based on the data flow. The following terms are important in interpreting scatter plots:

- **Trend line or regression line:** This line passes as closely as possible through the middle of the scattered points.

- **Positive correlation:** Correlation specifies the direction of the regression line and how closely the two variables correspond. With a positive correlation, the regression line has a positive slope; that is, the line rises from left to right.

- **Negative correlation:** The regression line has a negative slope; that is, the line runs downhill from left to right.

- **No correlation:** The points are simply scattered all over the graph so that a regression line can't clearly be determined.

- **Strong or weak correlation:** The closer the points are to the regression line, the stronger the correlation. Conversely, the farther they are from the line, the weaker the correlation.

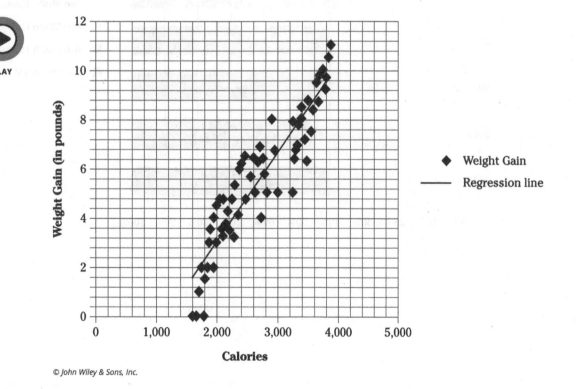

© *John Wiley & Sons, Inc.*

Based on the data in this scatter plot, about how many calories would need to be consumed to result in a 12-pound gain?

(A) 3,000

(B) 3,500

(C) 4,000

(D) 4,500

(E) 5,000

Lay your pencil on top of the regression line and follow it to see where it intersects the graph at 12 pounds. Use the grid to follow the line down to the x-axis, and you have your answer: about 4,500 calories. Correct answer: Choice (D).

Interpreting two graphs

Some graph questions on the GRE contain two graphs, usually of different types. To answer the questions, you may need to extract data from one or both graphs.

Here's an example:

Causes of Reduced College GPAs

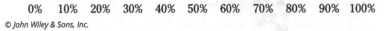

Legend:
- Too Much Football
- Too Much Golf
- Too Much Homework
- Too Much TV

Years: 2022, 2021, 2020, 2019, 2018

x-axis: 0% 10% 20% 30% 40% 50% 60% 70% 80% 90% 100%

© John Wiley & Sons, Inc.

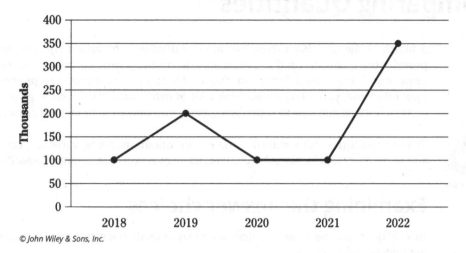

Number of Reduced College GPAs by Year

© John Wiley & Sons, Inc.

These two graphs are intended to be used in conjunction. The first graph is a bar graph that ranges from 0 to 100 percent. For this specific graph, calculate the impact of a cause of reduced GPAs by using the length of the bar segment. For example, for 2018, the Too Much Golf category (as a cause of reduced GPAs) begins at 10 percent and extends to 40 percent, for a range of 30 percent. If you say that in 2018, Too Much Golf was 40 percent, you're overlooking the 10-percent segment that is Too Much Football. Also, in 2022, Too Much Homework extends from 70 percent to 90 percent, for a range of 20 percent.

TIP

The second graph gives you the actual number of reduced GPAs in thousands. Be sure to look at the labels of the axes, which for the second graph says "Thousands." This means that in 2018, the GPAs of 100,000 study participants, not 100, went down.

Now, use the graphs together to find the number of students whose GPAs were reduced by a specific cause (or causes). For example, in 2019, 200,000 students had reduced GPAs. In that same year, Too Much Homework caused 20 percent of these reduced GPAs (from 50 to 70 percent). Twenty percent of 200,000 is 40,000 students who had reduced GPAs due to Too Much Homework.

Ready to try a practice question? Here you go:

PLAY

Which of the following represents the total number of college students from 2018 to 2022, inclusive?

(A) 850

(B) 8,500

(C) 85,000

(D) 850,000

(E) It cannot be determined from the information given.

Did you fall for the trap and pick Choice (D)? Because the graphs give you only the number of *reduced* GPAs (look at the titles of the graphs), you have no way to determine the total number of college students. The correct answer is Choice (E). Note that *inclusive* means that you include 2018 and 2022 (as opposed to "in between 2018 and 2022," which means you *don't* include those years).

TIP

Another tip when interpreting graphs: When choosing from answers that are far apart, consider rounding as you perform your calculations, especially if you're working with really big numbers and the question says "approximately" or "closest to."

Comparing Quantities

A bunch of the GRE Math questions are quantitative comparison (QC), meaning the question provides two quantities, and you answer by determining which is greater, or whether they're the same or you need more information. You need to recognize common setups and know the strategies; otherwise, you'll end up working a lot of extra math. This section gives you the lowdown on QC questions and how to solve them, along with how to steer clear of common pitfalls.

REMEMBER

The two quantities, aptly named A and B, can contain numbers, variables, equations, scenarios, and so on. Fortunately, like all GRE Math, these questions use common, specific setups.

Examining the answer choices

In a QC question, the answer choices are always exactly the same, so glance at them on test day, but understand them now:

(A) Quantity A is greater.

(B) Quantity B is greater.

(C) The two quantities are equal.

(D) The relationship cannot be determined from the information given.

You don't need to read and interpret these answer choices each time you see them. Instead, paraphrase them to make them simpler:

(A) A is greater.

(A) B is greater.

(A) They're equal.

(A) You need more info.

Understanding the basic steps

The best way to begin *most* QC questions is with a simple three-step approach:

1. Simplify Quantity A.

Simplify may mean solve the equation, read through a word problem, or estimate.

2. Simplify Quantity B.

Sometimes Quantity B is simpler than Quantity A, but not always. Sometimes a ballpark estimate is sufficient, as I show you later in this section.

3. Compare the two quantities.

At this point, you know which quantity is larger.

Here is a starter question to get you warmed up:

$$x < 0$$

Quantity A	**Quantity B**
x^2	x^3

(A) Quantity A is greater.

(B) Quantity B is greater.

(C) The two quantities are equal.

(D) The relationship cannot be determined from the information given.

All you know is that x is negative. How can you answer this question? Well, you don't *need* to know what x is. If it's negative, then squared, it becomes positive, so Quantity A is positive. Cubed, it stays negative, so Quantity B is negative. Pick a number to try it out. Say $x = -2$: Quantity A is $(-2)(-2) = 4$ and Quantity B is $(-2)(-2)(-2) = -8$. Regardless of what x is, it's negative, so Quantity A is greater. Correct answer: Choice (A).

TIP

This simple example highlights a key point regarding QC questions: Many are based on the *concept* of the math, not the math itself. If you know basic number properties, such as how negative numbers multiply out, you'll save yourself a lot of pencil work on these questions.

Understanding strategies for Quantity Comparison questions

With plenty of common setups and traps in the QC questions, I've included a separate section for each one, complete with examples and strategies for comparing them.

REMEMBER

Keep in mind that the following strategies aren't fail-safe. They *get you started*, but you still have to use your critical thinking, and when it makes sense, I include a practice question where the strategy alone doesn't do it. The GRE has far too many variations to anticipate them all, so never shut off your critical thinking in favor of a strategy.

Similar appearances

If Quantities A and B appear to be equal, don't fall for it — a trap is almost always involved. Treat them like they're similar. Check out the following example:

PLAY

Quantity A	**Quantity B**
2π	6.28

(A) Quantity A is greater.

(B) Quantity B is greater.

(C) The two quantities are equal.

(D) The relationship cannot be determined from the information given.

Your gut reaction may be to pick Choice (C) because both quantities appear to be equal at first glance. After all, wasn't it drilled into your head in school (and earlier in this block) that π is about 3.14, making 2π about 6.28? But hold the phone: The value of π is *slightly more* than 3.14. It's more like 3.1416, making π *greater than* 3.14 and 2π *greater than* 6.28, so Choice (A) is the right answer.

Drawings

Drawings in the GRE are typically drawn to scale, so you may be able to eyeball the correct answer. But if a figure contains the caveat "not drawn to scale," then it's *way* off. You can trust the right-angle box and that the angle touches the line on one point, as in this drawing, but you can't trust the dimensions.

PLAY

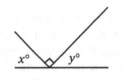

Note: Figure not drawn to scale.

Quantity A	Quantity B
x	y

(A) Quantity A is greater.

(B) Quantity B is greater.

(C) The two quantities are equal.

(D) The relationship cannot be determined from the information given.

Sure, x and y appear to be roughly 45 degrees each, but because the drawing isn't to scale, you can't make an estimate. You do know that x and y add up to 90 degrees because angles along a straight line add up to 180 degrees, and you already have a right angle: $180 - 90 = 90$. But you *don't* know how much of the 90 is x and how much is y. Correct answer: Choice (D).

REMEMBER

Even if this drawing *were* to scale, you couldn't look at x and y and assume they're equal. You can *estimate*, but that's all it is — an estimate. It could be that x is 46 and y is 44, for example.

Only two types of drawings are scaled for you to typically answer the question from the drawing itself: the xy-coordinate grid and the data graph, covered earlier in this block. Other than that, you need to confirm that the shape is what it looks like. If you see a square, but the GRE doesn't tell you that it's a square, you can't assume that the angles are 90° or that the side lengths are the same.

TIP

Concepts

Even though you can't always use the drawing to extract an exact measurement, you don't usually have to. The drawing tells you how the question is set up, and you *can* spot and use the math concepts.

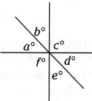

Quantity A	_Quantity B_
$a + b$	$d + e$

(A) Quantity A is greater.

(B) Quantity B is greater.

(C) The two quantities are equal.

(D) The relationship cannot be determined from the information given.

Angle *a* is *vertical* to angle *d*, meaning they're equal. Angle *b* is vertical to angle *e*, meaning they're also equal. Even though you can't tell the angle measures, you know these angle pairs are equal because of the math *concept*, and you can answer the question, regardless of whether the drawing is to scale. Because $a + b$ is equal to $d + e$, the quantities are equal, and the correct answer is Choice (C). See "Lines and angles" earlier in this block for a refresher.

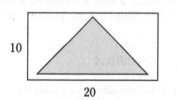

Quantity A	_Quantity B_
The area of the triangle	100

(A) Quantity A is greater.

(B) Quantity B is greater.

(C) The two quantities are equal.

(D) The relationship cannot be determined from the information given.

Don't pick Choice (D) just because you don't have the measurements of the triangle. Though the image isn't drawn to scale, you can use logic and critical thinking to compare the triangle to 100.

You know that the area of a triangle is $\frac{\text{base} \times \text{height}}{2}$. What's the base of this triangle? You can't tell, but you can see that the base of the triangle doesn't touch the sides of the rectangle, so it must be *less* than 20, which is the base of the rectangle. What's the height of this triangle? You can't tell that either, but you *can* see that it's less than 10, which is the height of the rectangle. Multiply less-than-10 by less-than-20 and divide that in half for less-than-100, making Quantity B greater and the correct answer Choice (B).

Identical terms

When the quantities have identical terms, clear out the clutter by canceling them out so you can focus on the parts that are different. After all, a QC problem is like a balance: If something is the same on both sides, it doesn't affect the balance, so you can ignore it. Be careful that you cancel only *identical* terms. For example, you can't cancel −5 from one side and 5 from the other.

PLAY

Quantity A	*Quantity B*
$x^2 - 21$	$x^2 - 35$

(A) Quantity A is greater.

(B) Quantity B is greater.

(C) The two quantities are equal.

(D) The relationship cannot be determined from the information given.

Cancel the x^2 in both quantities, and you're left with −21 and −35. Because −21 is greater than −35, the correct answer is Choice (A).

SORTING IDENTICAL TERMS

Sometimes the identical terms are masked within the question. You can't just eyeball them and cancel — you need to figure out the identical terms that you can cancel. Try out this example:

PLAY

Quantity A	*Quantity B*
The sum of all consecutive even integers from 14 to 28, inclusive.	The sum of all consecutive even integers from 18 to 30, inclusive.

(A) Quantity A is greater.

(B) Quantity B is greater.

(C) The two quantities are equal.

(D) The relationship cannot be determined from the information given.

Don't even *think* about adding up those numbers. What do the two quantities have in common that you can cancel? First, note that you *can't* cancel anything not on both sides: Only Quantity A has 14 and 16, while only Quantity B has 30. Because both quantities have 18, 20, 22, 24, 26, and 28, you can cancel those. Now the question looks like this:

>> Quantity A: 14+16

>> Quantity B: 30

To quote Billie Eilish: "Duh." The correct answer is Choice (C).

PLAY

Quantity A	_Quantity B_
The product of all consecutive integers from 10 to 109, inclusive.	The product of all consecutive integers from 12 to 110, inclusive.

(A) Quantity A is greater.

(B) Quantity B is greater.

(C) The two quantities are equal.

(D) The relationship cannot be determined from the information given.

Work all that math? Not a chance. Instead, focus your critical eye. Which numbers are on the left but not the right? 10 and 11. What's on the right but not the left? 110. The other numbers are identical, so cancel them out, and you're left with 110 on both sides because $10 \times 11 = 110$. Correct answer: Choice (C).

MAKING IDENTICAL TERMS

The GRE goes even further and masks the terms so they don't appear identical. What you do is *make* them identical, and *then* you can cancel them. This goes back to knowing the math concept.

PLAY

Quantity A	_Quantity B_
$79 \times 80 \times 81 \times 82$	80^4

(A) Quantity A is greater.

(B) Quantity B is greater.

(C) The two quantities are equal.

(D) The relationship cannot be determined from the information given.

Make the terms identical so you can cancel them. $80^4 = 80 \times 80 \times 80 \times 80$, so cancel the 80 from each side. Now you're left with this:

>> Quantity A: $79 \times 81 \times 82$

>> Quantity B: $80 \times 80 \times 80$

Even though it's simpler, still don't do that math. Though 79 in Quantity A is slightly less than 80 in Quantity B, the 81 and 82 in Quantity A are greater than the other two 80s in Quantity B, by a larger amount. Correct answer: Choice (A).

PLAY

Quantity A	_Quantity B_
$\dfrac{500!}{498!}$	499^2

(A) Quantity A is greater.

(B) Quantity B is greater.

(C) The two quantities are equal.

(D) The relationship cannot be determined from the information given.

Laughing yet? You will be. Remember how to divide factorials from earlier in this block: You cancel them out. Reduce Quantity A to $\frac{500 \times 499 \times 498!}{498!} = 500 \times 499$, while Quantity B is 499×499. Then cancel 499 from each side, making Quantities A and B into 500 and 499, respectively. Quantity A is greater. A not-too-bad correct answer: Choice (A).

Ranges

Sometimes the QC question tells you that x has a *range* of values. For example, it might tell you that x is between 2 and 10. Don't bother trying x as 4.5, 9.99, or any of the other dozens of numbers that it could be. You don't have all day. Just try x as the lowest and the highest that it could be. For example, when x is between 2 and 10, try $x = 2$ and $x = 10$, and you're done (usually).

PLAY

$$2 < x < 10$$

Quantity A	*Quantity B*
$\frac{x}{2}$	$2x$

(A) Quantity A is greater.

(B) Quantity B is greater.

(C) The two quantities are equal.

(D) The relationship cannot be determined from the information given.

First, try $x = 2$, making Quantity A equal 1 and Quantity B equal 4. Next, try $x = 10$, making Quantity A equal 5 and Quantity B equal 20. Either way, Quantity B is greater, and you don't have to try any other possible values of x for the correct answer of Choice (B).

Estimates

Pretend the QC problem is a balance scale, where you compare Quantity A to Quantity B. If Quantity A is heavier than Quantity B, Quantity A is greater.

PLAY

Quantity A	*Quantity B*
$\frac{17}{21} + \frac{47}{80}$	$\frac{19}{81} + \frac{23}{97}$

(A) Quantity A is greater.

(B) Quantity B is greater.

(C) The two quantities are equal.

(D) The relationship cannot be determined from the information given.

You don't need your pencil for this one. Compare each part of Quantity A to its counterpart in Quantity B. Whereas the Quantity A fractions are each more than one-half, the Quantity B fractions are each roughly a quarter, so they're less than one-half. Two more-than-halves on the left; two less-than-halves on the right. Correct answer: Choice (A).

The GRE is also testing how resourceful you are. Do you just blindly jump in and start working, or do you assess the elements and see if there's another way? Before working any math, check whether it's a trap that consumes your time.

Comparing with Four Square

When x or some other letter represents numbers, and there's no way to tell what these numbers are, one strategy is to use the *Four Square*: 2, -2, $\frac{1}{2}$, and $-\frac{1}{2}$. (You could use 0.5 and −0.5 instead of $\frac{1}{2}$ and $-\frac{1}{2}$.) The Four Square covers most possibilities, and you'll see whether the quantity that seems greater flips or stays the same.

Quantity A	*Quantity B*
x^2	x^4

(A) Quantity A is greater.

(B) Quantity B is greater.

(C) The two quantities are equal.

(D) The relationship cannot be determined from the information given.

Remember, both x's have the *same* value at any one time. The trap answer is Choice (B). Certainly a number to the fourth power is greater than the same number squared, right? Positive or negative, no matter.

But wait — what happens when you use the Four Square? Sure, 2 and −2 make Choice (B) seem correct, but $\frac{1}{2}$ and $-\frac{1}{2}$ make it Choice (A). Together, they make it a correct Choice (D).

You don't always have to go through the entire Four Square. As soon as two numbers give you two different answer choices, you can stop. In this example, just trying 2 and $\frac{1}{2}$ would have done the trick.

If you happen to find that the quantities could be equal *or* one could be greater, don't go with the one that could be greater — go with Choice (D).

Comparing with a hundred

If a question deals with dollars or percentages, start with 100 to make it an easier number. Remember that the key is simplifying the math.

A book bag costs x dollars.

Quantity A	*Quantity B*
Cost of the book bag on sale at 60% off	$0.6x$

(A) Quantity A is greater.

(B) Quantity B is greater.

(C) The two quantities are equal.

(D) The relationship cannot be determined from the information given.

If you make $x = \$100$, you can easily determine that 60 percent of 100 is 60; subtract 60 from 100, and you get 40. In Quantity B, $0.6(100) = 60$. The answer is Choice (B).

REMEMBER

This type of problem is easy to miss because of carelessness. Other test-takers automatically opt for Choice (C), but not you. When both sides have a percent of x, start with 100 for x and do the math.

Comparing multiple unknowns

Some questions may provide you with multiple unknowns. In that case, try numbers that are close together and then numbers that are far apart. For example, with three unknowns, try consecutive numbers such as 1, 2, and 3, and then try spread-out numbers such as 2, 5, and 200. If this doesn't change which quantity is greater, you could try negative numbers. On these questions, you can usually skip trying fractions.

PLAY

$$x > y > z$$

Quantity A	Quantity B
$y + z$	x

(A) Quantity A is greater.

(B) Quantity B is greater.

(C) The two quantities are equal.

(D) The relationship cannot be determined from the information given.

The trap answer is Choice (C), but you know better. Because x, y, and z can be anything, the right answer is *probably* Choice (D), but try it out just to be sure. Start with 3, 2, and 1 for x, y, and z, respectively. Quantity A is $2 + 1$ and Quantity B is 3, making them equal. But when you mix it up with very different numbers — say, 100, 5, and 1 — Quantity A is $y + z = 5 + 1 = 6$, and Quantity B, x, is 100, making Quantity B larger. Because you're able to change the correct answer, go with Choice (D).

Block 4
Taking a Shortened Practice Test

You're now ready to take a practice GRE. Although this practice test is shortened to 1.5 hours so you can prepare for the whole exam in 5 hours, you can take this practice test under normal exam conditions and approach it as you would the real GRE:

TIP

>> **Work when you won't be interrupted.** Pick a quiet time of day when there are fewer opportunities for distraction.

>> **Use scratch paper that's free of any prepared notes.** On the actual GRE, you receive blank scratch paper before your test begins.

>> **Answer as many questions as time allows.** Consider answering all the easier questions within each section first and then going back to answer the harder questions. Because you're not penalized for guessing, go ahead and guess on the remaining questions before time expires.

>> **Set a timer for each section and don't leave your desk.** In this shortened format, you have 30 minutes for the essay, 40 minutes for the math, and 20 minutes for the verbal. If you have time left at the end, you may go back and review answers (within the section), continue and finish your test early, or pause and catch your mental breath before moving on to the next section.

>> **Type the essays.** Because you type the essays on the actual GRE, typing them now is good practice. Don't use software that checks spelling and grammar, such as Microsoft Word. Instead, use a simple text editor, such as Notepad. The GRE essay-writing space features undo, redo, copy, and paste functionality — but nothing else.

After completing this practice test, go to the end of this block to check your answers. Be sure to review the explanations for *all* the questions, not just the ones you missed. The answer explanations provide insight and a review of the material you went over in the previous chapters. This way, you also review the explanations for questions you weren't sure of.

REMEMBER

If you're taking the computerized GRE, the answer choices aren't marked with A, B, C, D, E, and F. Instead, they have clickable ovals and check boxes, boxes where you type in numeric answers, and click-a-sentence options (for some Reading Comprehension questions). Here, the questions and answer choices are formatted to challenge you in the same way and build the same skills that you'll use on test day.

Answer Sheet for Practice Exam

Section 1:
Verbal Reasoning

1. Ⓐ Ⓑ Ⓒ Ⓓ Ⓔ
2. Ⓐ Ⓑ Ⓒ Ⓓ Ⓔ
3. Ⓐ Ⓑ Ⓒ Ⓓ Ⓔ Ⓕ
4. Ⓐ Ⓑ Ⓒ Ⓓ Ⓔ Ⓕ
5. Ⓐ Ⓑ Ⓒ Ⓓ Ⓔ Ⓕ Ⓖ Ⓗ Ⓘ
6. Ⓐ Ⓑ Ⓒ Ⓓ Ⓔ Ⓕ Ⓖ Ⓗ Ⓘ
7. Ⓐ Ⓑ Ⓒ Ⓓ Ⓔ
8. A B C D E
9. A B C
10. A B C
11. Ⓐ Ⓑ Ⓒ Ⓓ Ⓔ
12. A B C
13. Ⓐ Ⓑ Ⓒ Ⓓ Ⓔ
14. Ⓐ Ⓑ Ⓒ Ⓓ Ⓔ
15. Ⓐ Ⓑ Ⓒ Ⓓ Ⓔ
16. Ⓐ Ⓑ Ⓒ Ⓓ Ⓔ
17. A B C D E F
18. A B C D E F
19. A B C D E F
20. A B C D E F

Section 2:
Quantitative Reasoning

1. Ⓐ Ⓑ Ⓒ Ⓓ Ⓔ
2. Ⓐ Ⓑ Ⓒ Ⓓ Ⓔ
3. A B C D E
4. Ⓐ Ⓑ Ⓒ Ⓓ
5. Ⓐ Ⓑ Ⓒ Ⓓ
6. Ⓐ Ⓑ Ⓒ Ⓓ
7. Ⓐ Ⓑ Ⓒ Ⓓ
8. Ⓐ Ⓑ Ⓒ Ⓓ
9. Ⓐ Ⓑ Ⓒ Ⓓ
10. Ⓐ Ⓑ Ⓒ Ⓓ
11. Ⓐ Ⓑ Ⓒ Ⓓ Ⓔ
12. Ⓐ Ⓑ Ⓒ Ⓓ Ⓔ
13. Ⓐ Ⓑ Ⓒ Ⓓ Ⓔ
14. A B C
15. ☐
16. ☐
17. A B C D E F
18. Ⓐ Ⓑ Ⓒ Ⓓ Ⓔ
19. ☐
20. A B C D E F

Analytical Writing: Analyze an Issue

TIME: 30 minutes

Oversight of media and personal expression is an important part of any mature society.

DIRECTIONS: Write a response in which you express the extent to which you agree or disagree with the preceding statement and explain the reasoning behind your position. In support of your position, think of ways in which the statement may or may not be true and how these considerations influence your position.

Section 1

Verbal Reasoning

TIME: 20 minutes for 20 questions

DIRECTIONS: Choose the best answer to each question. Blacken the corresponding ovals or boxes on the answer sheet.

Directions: For Questions 1–7, choose the one entry best suited for each blank from its corresponding column of choices.

1. Corporate leaders often try to _____ their intentions, as disclosing the motives that drive decisions may put the company's strategic advantage at risk.

Ⓐ occlude
Ⓑ stipulate
Ⓒ obfuscate
Ⓓ preclude
Ⓔ abjure

2. Refusing to consider criticism, however valid, may lead an individual in a position of power to suffer from one's own _____, leading to decisions that ultimately produce catastrophic results.

Ⓐ miscalculations
Ⓑ ambivalence
Ⓒ perfidy
Ⓓ ineptitude
Ⓔ hubris

3. Many observers of the trial believed that the judge's (i) _____ of the prosecutor for misconduct, after which the prosecutor appeared despondent, ultimately led to the defendant's (ii) _____.

Blank (i)	Blank (ii)
Ⓐ adjudication	Ⓓ conviction
Ⓑ excoriation	Ⓔ deposition
Ⓒ exoneration	Ⓕ exoneration

4. The report, (i) _____ from the company's own internal documents, revealed that its network was in fact not (ii) _____.

Blank (i)	Blank (ii)
Ⓐ coerced	Ⓓ vulnerable
Ⓑ gleaned	Ⓔ implacable
Ⓒ redacted	Ⓕ impregnable

5. A (i) _____ democracy must be built on certain (ii) _____ in order to survive. Giving the populace the right to vote without establishing the rule of law makes a young democracy (iii) _____ to devolving into a dictatorship.

Blank (i)	Blank (ii)	Blank (iii)
Ⓐ well-established	Ⓓ precepts	Ⓖ dedicated
Ⓑ nascent	Ⓔ criteria	Ⓗ resolute
Ⓒ representative	Ⓕ precedents	Ⓘ prone

6. A curved mirror produces an optical (i) _____ — a (ii) _____ in the appearance of the object it reflects. While looking in such a mirror may amuse some, others may find it (iii) _____.

Blank (i)	Blank (ii)	Blank (iii)
Ⓐ vacillation	Ⓓ distortion	Ⓖ debilitating
Ⓑ aberration	Ⓔ divergence	Ⓗ humorous
Ⓒ translucence	Ⓕ detraction	Ⓘ discomfiting

GO ON TO NEXT PAGE

Directions: Each of the following passages is followed by questions pertaining to the passage. Read the passage and answer the questions based on information stated or implied in that passage. For each question, select one answer choice unless instructed otherwise.

The following passage is an excerpt from The Role of the Father in Childhood Development, 5th Edition, by Michael E. Lamb, editor (Wiley).

Whether and how much time fathers spend with their children are questions at the heart of much research conducted over the past three decades. In the mid-1970s a number of investigators sought to describe — often by detailed observation and sometimes also through detailed maternal and paternal reports — the extent of paternal interactions with children (Pleck & Masciadrelli, this volume; Lamb & Lewis, this volume). Many of these researchers have framed their research around the three types of paternal involvement (engagement, accessibility, responsibility) described by Lamb, Pleck, Charnov, and Levine (1987). As Pleck and Masciadrelli note, researchers have consistently shown that fathers spend much less time with their children than do mothers. In two-parent families in which mothers are unemployed, fathers spend about one-fourth as much time as mothers in direct interaction or engagement with their children, and about a third as much time being accessible to their children. Many fathers assume essentially no responsibility (as defined by participation in key decisions, availability at short notice, involvement in the care of sick children, management and selection of alternative child care, etc.) for their children's care or rearing, however, and the small subgroup of fathers who assume high degrees of responsibility has not been studied extensively. Average levels of paternal responsibility have increased over time, albeit slowly, and there appear to be small but continuing increases over time in average levels of all types of parental involvement.

7. Which sentence most clearly summarizes the research supporting the primary conclusion stated in this article?

(A) Whether and how much time fathers spend with their children are questions at the heart of much research conducted over the past three decades.

(B) Many of these researchers have framed their research around the three types of paternal involvement (engagement, accessibility, responsibility) described by Lamb, Pleck, Charnov, and Levine (1987).

(C) As Pleck and Masciadrelli note, researchers have consistently shown that fathers spend much less time with their children than do mothers.

(D) In two-parent families in which mothers are unemployed, fathers spend about one-fourth as much time as mothers in direct interaction or engagement with their children, and about a third as much time being accessible to their children.

(E) Average levels of paternal responsibility have increased over time, albeit slowly, and there appear to be small but continuing increases over time in average levels of all types of parental involvement.

For Questions 8, 9, and 10, consider each answer choice separately and select all answer choices that are correct.

8. As defined in the paragraph, which of the following would not constitute "paternal responsibility"?

(A) Taking care of a child who is ill

(B) Reading to a child

(C) Choosing a childcare provider

(D) Providing food, clothing, and housing for a child

(E) Playing a game with a child

9. Data from which of the following were not included in the research?

(A) Single-parent families

(B) Two-parent families in which the fathers are unemployed

(C) Two-parent families in which the mothers are unemployed

10. Which of the following did researchers use as a measure of paternal involvement or responsibility?

(A) Engagement, accessibility, and the care of sick children

(B) Accessibility, responsibility, and financial support

(C) Engagement and availability at short notice

The following passage is an excerpt from World Literature in Theory *by David Damrosch, editor (Wiley-Blackwell).*

What are we to make of world literature today? The cultural and political realignments of the past two decades have opened the field of world literature to an unprecedented, even <u>vertiginous</u> variety of authors and countries. At once exhilarating and unsettling, the range and variety of literatures now in view raise serious questions of scale, of translation and comprehension, and of persisting imbalances of economic and cultural power. At the same time, the shifting landscape of world literature offers new opportunities for readers to encounter writers located well beyond the select few western European countries whose works long dominated worldwide attention. Whereas in past eras works usually spread from imperial centers to peripheral regions (from China to Vietnam, from London to Australia and Kenya, from Paris to almost everywhere), an increasingly multipolar literary landscape allows writers from smaller countries to achieve rapid worldwide fame. While still in his fifties, Orhan Pamuk became the second-youngest recipient of the Nobel Prize for Literature and was translated into 56 languages, Vietnamese included; he has many more readers abroad than in his native Turkey. Increasingly complex patterns of travel, emigration, and publication make "national" languages and literatures more and more international in character. The winner of the Nobel Prize in 2000, Gao Xingjian, has long lived in France and has become a French citizen, yet he continues to write in Chinese. Cultural hybridity is also found within the borders of China itself, as in the stories of the Sino-Tibetan writer Tashi Dawa, who has blended elements drawn from Tibetan folklore and international magical realism for his writings in Chinese; in a very real sense, his works were participating in world literature even before they began to be translated and read abroad.

11. In the context in which it appears, "vertiginous" most nearly means

    (A) Conceivable
    (B) Plausible
    (C) Dizzying
    (D) Enlightening
    (E) Edifying

For Question 12, consider each answer choice separately and select all answer choices that are correct.

12. Which of the following is/are given as example(s) of cross-cultural influence in literature?

    (A) Distributing literary works from London to Kenya
    (B) A French citizen writing in Chinese
    (C) Blending magical realism with Tibetan folklore

The following passage is an excerpt from Sensory Evaluation: A Practical Handbook *by Susan Kemp, Tracey Hollowood, and Joanne Hort (Wiley-Blackwell).*

<u>Volatile</u> molecules are sensed by olfactory receptors on the millions of hair-like cilia that cover the nasal epithelium (located in the roof of the nasal cavity). Consequently, for something to have an odour or aroma, volatile molecules must be transported in air to the nose. Volatile molecules enter the nose orthonasally during breathing/sniffing, or retronasally via the back of the throat during eating. There are around 17,000 different volatile compounds. A particular odour may be made up of several volatile compounds, but sometimes particular volatiles (character-impact compounds) can be associated with a particular smell, e.g., iso-amyl acetate and banana/pear drops. Individuals may perceive and/or describe single compounds differently, e.g., hexenol can be described as grass, green, unripe. Similarly, an odour quality may be perceived and/or described in different compounds, e.g., minty is used to describe both menthol and carvone.

13. Which of the following is not mentioned as a reason that associating an odor with a specific volatile compound may be difficult?

    (A) Several volatiles may contribute to producing a specific odor.
    (B) People may perceive the odor of compounds differently.
    (C) A character-impact compound can be associated with a particular smell.
    (D) The odors of different compounds may be perceived or described as having the same quality.
    (E) People may describe the odor of compounds differently.

GO ON TO NEXT PAGE

14. In the context in which it appears, "volatile" most nearly means

(A) Explosive

(B) Evaporating rapidly

(C) Fleeting; transient

(D) Fluctuating rapidly

(E) Changeable

Typical silt loam soil is comprised of approximately 50 percent soil particles, 25 percent water, and 25 percent air. **Heavy farm equipment compacts the soil, significantly reducing the amount of air and water it can store and inhibiting the movement of air and water through the soil.** Soil compaction reduces crop yields in several ways. It impedes root penetration, reduces the amount of beneficial bacteria and fungi in the soil, increases the potential for runoff and soil erosion, reduces nutrient uptake, and stunts plant growth. To reduce soil compaction, **farmers are advised to avoid trafficking on wet soil, avoid using oversized equipment, reduce axle loads, limit tilling, and increase the soil's organic matter content.**

15. In this passage, the bolded portions play which of the following roles?

(A) The first states a conclusion; the second provides evidence to support that conclusion.

(B) The first states a problem, the effects of which are detailed in the second.

(C) The first states a conclusion that the second provides evidence to oppose.

(D) The first serves as an intermediate conclusion that supports a further conclusion stated in the second.

(E) The first offers a supposition that is countered by the guidance in the second.

Since 1985, California's lottery has contributed more than $24 billion to public schools, including some $19 billion for K–12 schools. In this way, state lotteries increase revenue for education.

16. Which of the following, if true, most seriously undermines the argument?

(A) In states without lotteries, citizens often cross the state line to play the lottery in a neighboring state.

(B) The California Lottery is required to provide at least 34 percent of its revenues to public education.

(C) The South Dakota Lottery has provided more than $1.7 billion to the Property Tax Reduction Fund.

(D) Lottery revenue represents less than 5 percent of the total education budget in states that use lottery revenue for education.

(E) Many states divert lottery dollars from their K–12 education programs to their general funds to make up for shortfalls.

Directions: Each of the following sentences has a blank indicating that a word or phrase is omitted. Choose the two answers that best complete the sentence and result in two sentences most alike in meaning.

17. Though exhausted, the victor remained _____ during his speech.

(A) vivacious

(B) lugubrious

(C) ebullient

(D) laconic

(E) mendacious

(F) disingenuous

18. Con artists have been known to file _____ quitclaim deeds, which transfer ownership of the house from the victim to the perpetrator.

(A) extenuated

(B) inadvertent

(C) counterfeit

(D) exculpated

(E) pilfered

(F) spurious

19. In the United States, to protect young viewers, the Federal Communications Commission (FCC) enforces laws that prohibit the broadcast of certain images and language during certain hours, but it has had no success in restricting content that glorifies _____.

(A) truculence

(B) turpitude

(C) asperity

(D) infidelity

(E) depravity

(F) impertinence

20. The keynote speaker was incredibly _____, exceeding her allotted time by more than 45 minutes.

(A) eloquent

(B) loquacious

(C) voluble

(D) vivacious

(E) voluminous

(F) articulate

DO NOT TURN THE PAGE UNTIL TOLD TO DO SO **STOP** DO NOT RETURN TO A PREVIOUS TEST

Section 2
Quantitative Reasoning

TIME: 40 minutes for 20 questions

NOTES:

- All numbers used in this exam are real numbers.

- All figures lie in a plane.

- Angle measures are positive; points and angles are in the position shown.

1. $\dfrac{5\left(2^{12}\right)}{4^{5}} =$

   (A) 5
   (B) 10
   (C) 15
   (D) 20
   (E) 25

2. If y is an integer and $\sqrt{48y}$ is an integer, which of the following is the lowest possible value of y?

   (A) 1
   (B) 2
   (C) 3
   (D) 4
   (E) 6

3. If n is an integer and $\dfrac{210}{n}$ is an integer, which of the following could be the value of n? Indicate <u>all</u> such values.

   (A) 6
   (B) 12
   (C) 14
   (D) 35
   (E) 42

Directions: For Questions 4–10, choose from the following answers:

(A) *Quantity A is greater.*
(B) *Quantity B is greater.*
(C) *The two quantities are equal.*
(D) *The relationship cannot be determined from the information given.*

4. Fifteen candies are to be divided up among six children so that each child receives at least two candies.

Quantity A	_Quantity B_
The probability that any child receives six candies	0

5. Davis travels at a constant speed of 40 miles per hour for two hours and then at a constant speed of 60 miles per hour for one hour.

Quantity A	_Quantity B_
Davis's average speed for the entire trip	45 miles per hour

6.

Quantity A	_Quantity B_
900	$\sqrt{(30)(30)(30)(30)}$

7. $f(x) = x^2 + 2x - 2$

Quantity A	_Quantity B_
The value of x when $f(x)=13$	3

8.

Quantity A	_Quantity B_
$(0.99)^{99}$	1

9.

Quantity A	_Quantity B_
5!	$\dfrac{6!}{3!}$

10. A right circular cylinder has a volume of 36π.

Quantity A	_Quantity B_
The sum of the radius and height of the cylinder if the radius and height are both integers greater than 1	12

Questions 11–13 are based on the following graphs.

Physics Grades and Enrollments of Middle School Students in the Fraser School District Enrollment

		6th Grade	7th Grade	8th Grade	Totals
Subdistrict	Aguilar	83	99	89	271
	Bayfield	107	103	96	306
	Creede	74	70	67	211
	De Beque	40	36	39	115
	Eaton	69	64	69	202
	Totals	373	372	360	1,105

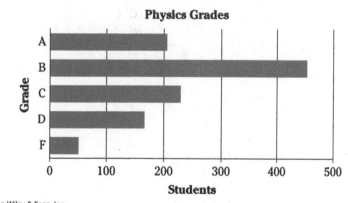

Physics Grades

11. What is the approximate ratio of students earning a C to those earning a B?

(A) 1:2

(B) 2:1

(C) 3:2

(D) 4:3

(E) 1:1

12. If all the students from Creede, and only those students, are earning A's and the rest of the grades are evenly distributed among students in the other subdistricts, approximately how many students from Bayfield are earning B's?

(A) 50

(B) 75

(C) 150

(D) 225

(E) 306

13. If all the grades are evenly distributed throughout all districts and classes, approximately how many students in De Beque are *not* earning a B?

(A) 20

(B) 40

(C) 70

(D) 100

(E) 115

14. If the range of set S is 9 and $S = \{2, 4, 5, 7, 8, 9, x\}$, which of the following *could* be the median of set S?

Indicate <u>all</u> possible answers.

(A) 5

(B) 6

(C) 7

15. $\left(\dfrac{1}{8} - \dfrac{3}{10}\right) + \left(\dfrac{1}{4} - \dfrac{1}{5}\right) + \left(\dfrac{5}{8} - \dfrac{1}{2}\right) =$

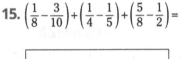

16. $\sqrt{9(36) + 12(36) + 15(36)} =$

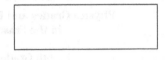

17. Given the inequality $x^2 < 25$, which of the following *could* be the value of x?

Indicate <u>all</u> such values.

(A) −6

(B) −5

(C) −3

(D) 0

(E) 3

(F) 5

18.

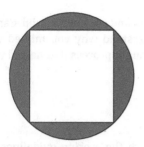

© John Wiley & Sons, Inc.

The square is inscribed within the circle and has a side length of $\sqrt{2}$. What is the area of the shaded portion of the drawing?

(A) $2 - \pi$

(B) $\pi - 2$

(C) $\pi - \sqrt{2}$

(D) $\pi - 4$

(E) $4 - \pi$

19.

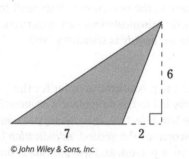

© John Wiley & Sons, Inc.

The area of the shaded triangle is

---

20. If Clarissa's monthly mortgage payment is less than $\frac{1}{3}$ but more than $\frac{1}{4}$ of her monthly income, and if the monthly mortgage payment is $600, which of the following could <u>not</u> be her annual income?

Indicate <u>all</u> such values.

(A) $12,200

(B) $17,400

(C) $21,000

(D) $24,200

(E) $29,000

(F) $31,300

Answers and Explanations

After taking the practice exam, use this section to check your answers and see how you did. Carefully review the explanations because doing so can help you understand why you missed the questions you did and also give you a better understanding of the thought process that helped you select the correct answers.

Analytical writing section

Have a friend or tutor read your essay: Refer that helpful person to the scoring guidelines in Block 2. If the essay is clear, persuasive, and grammatically sound, you probably got it.

Section 1: Verbal reasoning

1. **C.** Corporate leaders would try to *obfuscate* (conceal) their intentions in order to maintain a competitive advantage. *Occlude* makes a good runner-up, but it carries a meaning more along the lines of blocking off access to something. None of the other three choices is close: *Stipulate* means to demand something specific, *preclude* means to prevent or prohibit, and *abjure* means to avoid or reject.

2. **E.** *Hubris* is excessive pride or self-confidence, which is often characterized by a refusal to consider any criticism, as expressed in the opening phrase of the sentence. If it weren't for that qualifier, any of the other answer choices would work: *Miscalculations* can undermine a leader's plans, *ambivalence* is uncertainty or indecisiveness, *perfidy* is treachery, and *ineptitude* is incompetence.

3. **B, F.** The judge must have *excoriated* (severely criticized) the prosecutor in order for the prosecutor to be despondent, and that despondency likely led to the defendant's *exoneration* (acquittal) because the despondent prosecutor would be less effective. Otherwise, you could make a case for *exoneration* for the first blank and *conviction* for the second. *Adjudication* (a court order) is a legal term, but a judge doesn't adjudicate a person, and a *deposition* is done by a witness, not a defendant.

4. **B, F.** The report would have been *gleaned* (gathered) from internal documents, not *coerced* (gotten by force) or *redacted* (put into a suitable literary form). A company network is typically secure; the transition *in fact* tells you that's not the case here. Therefore, the network wasn't *impregnable* (able to withstand attack). *Vulnerable* would imply that security was stronger than IT thought. *Implacable* means unable to be satisfied or appeased.

5. **B, D, I.** The second sentence references a democracy in early development, so it must be a *nascent* (emerging) democracy that would need to be built on certain *precepts* (principles or guidelines) in order to be strong. Otherwise, the government would be *prone* (disposed to) to devolving into a dictatorship.

   For the first blank, you can rule out *well-established*, which is the opposite of *nascent*, and *representative*, which is just a type of democracy (direct or representative). For the second blank, both *criteria* and *precedents* would be good second choices, but because the second sentence mentions the right to vote and the rule of law, *precepts* is more accurate. *Criteria* also refers to qualifications, which doesn't fit. For the third blank, you can rule out *dedicated* because no democracy dedicates itself to becoming a dictatorship. You can rule out *resolute* (determined) for much the same reason.

6. **B, D, I.** The reflection in a curved mirror would be an *aberration* (an abnormality), not a *vacillation* (wavering) or *translucence* (semi-transparency), so the reflection in the mirror would be a *distortion* (misrepresentation). For the second blank, *divergence* (deviation or departure) would be a good second choice, but *distortion* is more precise. *Detraction* (disparagement or denigration) doesn't work. Some people find such a distorted reflection of themselves *discomfiting* (unsettling). *Debilitating* (incapacitating) is too strong a word, and *humorous* doesn't work because the last sentence is structured in a way that the missing word must be nearly the opposite of *amusing*.

7. **C.** You may be tempted to select the last sentence because it presents a summary of the data, but the main conclusion in this passage is that fathers spend considerably less time with their children than do mothers.

8. **B, D, E.** The paragraph defines paternal responsibility as "participation in key decisions, availability at short notice, involvement in the care of sick children, management and selection of alternative child care." Choice (D), food, clothing, and housing, may be considered "key decisions" as a stretch; Choice (B), reading, and Choice (E), playing a game, may be considered involvement, but the other choices clearly fall under the paragraph's definition of paternal responsibility.

9. **A, B.** The passage focuses on two-parent families in which mothers are unemployed and only mentions "the small subgroup of fathers who assume high degrees of responsibility." It doesn't provide data related to single-parent families or two-parent families in which the father stays home with the children.

10. **A, C.** Researchers did not include financial support as a measure of parental responsibility, so you can rule out answer Choice (B). Engagement, accessibility, availability at short notice, and the care of sick children are all mentioned as measures of parental responsibility.

11. **C.** *Vertiginous* means spinning, whirling — movement that would cause someone to become dizzy. Because this passage describes the variety of literature as overwhelming, in both positive and negative ways, the variety of authors and countries is considered vertiginous. You can immediately rule out the first two options, which both mean something along the lines of believable. Although literature may be *enlightening* (informative) and *edifying* (intellectually enriching), the *variety* of authors and countries would probably not be considered enlightening or edifying in this context.

12. **B, C.** Gao Xingjian is mentioned as a French citizen who continues to write in Chinese, while Tashi Dawa blends elements drawn from Tibetan folklore and international magical realism for his writings in Chinese. This question is a little tricky because cultural hybridity isn't mentioned until the second example of it is presented. Choice (A) is wrong because in this passage, *cultural hybridity* refers to the blending of cultures within a literary work, not the exchange of literary works between countries or cultures, although such exchanges no doubt promote cultural hybridity in literature.

13. **C.** The fact that a character-impact compound can be associated with a particular smell would help, not hinder, the ability to associate an odor with a specific volatile compound.

14. **B.** All the answer choices are definitions of *volatile,* but because the passage discusses molecules being distributed through the air, *evaporating rapidly* is the most accurate meaning.

15. **D.** The first bolded portion states the conclusion that heavy farm equipment compacts the soil, and the second bolded portion concludes that farmers must employ various strategies to reduce soil compaction. You can rule out Choice (A) because although the first states a conclusion, the second doesn't provide supporting evidence. Rule out Choice (B) because although the first states a problem, the second describes a possible solution to the problem, not the effects of that problem. Rule out Choices (C) and (E) because the second bolded portion doesn't oppose or counter the first.

16. **E.** This argument assumes that other states operate the same way as California. Choice (E) says, however, that other states divert monies from schools, which means that the lottery money doesn't actually increase revenue for education: Any money coming in from the lottery would be diverted away from education. Choices (A) and (C) are out of scope, while Choice (B) supports the argument, and (D) simply asserts that lottery funding represents a small portion of the total education budget in a state.

17. **A, C.** The victor was exhausted, but the transition *though* tells you that he behaved the opposite during his speech: *vivacious* (energetic) and *ebullient* (enthusiastic). You can easily rule out *lugubrious,* which means sad or gloomy; *laconic,* which means terse or concise; and *mendacious* and *disingenuous,* both meaning dishonest.

18. **C, F.** The deeds described here would be fake — *counterfeit* or *spurious. Extenuated* means severe and explained, as in *extenuating circumstance, inadvertent* means unintentional, and *exculpated* means freed from blame. *Pilfered* means stolen, but there is no other answer choice with a similar meaning, and anyway, filing a stolen deed wouldn't help the con artist transfer ownership of the property — it would have the true owner's name on it.

19. **B, E.** Think of something broadcast that can be harmful to young viewers but cannot be easily regulated. Because *turpitude* and *depravity* both mean immorality, and the passage focuses on indecent programming, these two choices are best. *Truculence* and *impertinence* both imply disrespectful behavior, but in a way that's not particularly harmful to youth. *Asperity,* which means harshness or sternness, has no choice comparable in meaning. Choice (D), *infidelity,* is tempting, but it doesn't have a match in the answer choices.

20. **B, C.** If the speaker exceeded her allotted time, she must have been *loquacious* or *voluble,* which both imply long-winded. She may have also been *eloquent* and *articulate* (well-spoken), but that wouldn't necessarily cause her to exceed her allotted speaking time. *Vivacious* means lively or energetic, and *voluminous* means large, neither of which has a comparable word in the list of answer choices and neither of which would necessarily cause the keynote speaker to run past her allotted time.

Section 2: Quantitative reasoning

1. **D.** First, convert the 4^5 into $\left(2^2\right)^5$, which becomes 2^{10}. Then simplify the fraction by subtracting the exponents:

$$\frac{5\left(2^{12}\right)}{4^5} = \frac{5\left(2^{12}\right)}{2^{10}} = 5\left(2^2\right) = 5(4) = 20$$

2. **C.** Factor the $\sqrt{48y}$ into $\sqrt{4 \times 4 \times 3 \times y}$. The lowest possible value of y is 3, because in order for the square root of $48y$ to be an integer, the factors inside the square root must form numbers squared. You have 4×4, and you need another 3 to match the existing 3 for 3×3 inside the radical.

   You could also try the answer choices, starting with the lowest value and working your way up: $\sqrt{48 \times 1} = \sqrt{48}$, which isn't an integer. $\sqrt{48 \times 2} = \sqrt{96}$, which isn't an integer. $\sqrt{48 \times 3} = \sqrt{144} = 12$, which is an integer. Factoring is faster, though.

3. **A, C, D, E.** $210 = 2 \times 3 \times 5 \times 7$, so n could be any product of 2, 3, 5, and 7, as long as each factor is used only once. 12 is wrong because it uses the factor 2 twice.

   You could also solve this one by trying answer choices, but that's a lot of math.

4. **C.** Regardless of the distribution, no child will receive six candies. After you give each child two candies, three candies are left over. If these are given to one child, the child will have a total of five.

5. **A.** You can find the average speed by placing the entire distance over the entire time. If Davis travels at 40 miles per hour for two hours, he travels 80 miles during that time. Combine this with 60 miles for one hour for a total of 140 miles in three hours:

$$\frac{140 \text{ miles}}{3 \text{ hours}} = \frac{47 \text{ miles}}{1 \text{ hour}}$$

6. **C.** Simplify the radical:

$$\sqrt{(30)(30)(30)(30)} = (30)(30) = 900$$

7. **D.** Given that $f(x) = x^2 + 2x - 2$ and $f(x) = 13$, set up and simplify the equation with 13 as $f(x)$:

$$
\begin{aligned}
f(x) &= x^2 + 2x - 2 \\
13 &= x^2 + 2x - 2 \\
0 &= x^2 + 2x - 15 \\
0 &= (x-3)(x+5)
\end{aligned}
$$

   Therefore, $x = 3$ or -5, but you don't know which one, so Quantity A could be either equal to or less than Quantity B. Because you don't know, go with Choice (D).

8. **B.** Any number between 0 and 1 becomes smaller when multiplied by itself. For example:

$$\left(\frac{1}{2}\right)^2 = \frac{1}{4}$$

Each time you multiply 0.99 by itself, the quantity becomes smaller and remains less than 1.

9. **C.** Simplify the factorial expressions:

$$5! = 5 \times 4 \times 3 \times 2 = 120$$

$$\frac{6!}{3!} = \frac{6 \times 5 \times 4 \times 3 \times 2}{3 \times 2} = 120$$

10. **B.** You can find the volume of a right circular cylinder with $\pi r^2 h$, where r is the radius and h is the height. If r and h are integers, the only way the volume can be 36π is if r is 3 and h is 4, with a sum of 7, or r is 2 and h is 9, with a sum of 11. Either way, the sum is less than 12.

11. **A.** The question asks for an "approximate" ratio, so eyeball the graph and compare the bars. The C bar is half the B bar, making the ratio 1:2.

12. **C.** If the 211 Creede students are earning A's, the remaining 894 students are earning all the other grades. Looking at the bar chart, the B bar is the length of the C, D, and F bars put together. This means that about half the remaining students are earning B's. Bayfield has 306 students, so approximately half that is 150.

13. **C.** From the bar chart, you can see that about $\frac{2}{5}$ of the grades are B grades, so about $\frac{3}{5}$ are the other grades. De Beque has 115 students, and the only answer choice that's about $\frac{3}{5}$ of that is 70.

    An estimate is usually good enough for these questions. The answer 70 isn't really close to the other answers, so if you eyeball the graph differently, you'll still get the right answer.

14. **A, C.** The range is the difference between the lowest and highest numbers. If the range of set S is 9 and none of the given numbers are 9 apart, x has to be either 0 or 11.

    The median is the middle number of the set. If x is 0, the median is 5; if x is 11, the median is 7.

15. **0.** The trap here is doing a lot of extra math work. Drop the parentheses to avoid this trap:

$$\frac{1}{8} - \frac{3}{10} + \frac{1}{4} - \frac{1}{5} + \frac{5}{8} - \frac{1}{2}$$

Now give the fractions common denominators of either 8 or 10:

$$\frac{1}{8} - \frac{3}{10} + \frac{2}{8} - \frac{2}{10} + \frac{5}{8} - \frac{5}{10}$$

The $\frac{1}{8}$, $\frac{2}{8}$, and $\frac{5}{8}$ add up to 1, and the $-\frac{3}{10}$, $-\frac{2}{10}$, and $-\frac{5}{10}$ add up to -1. The sum, therefore, equals 0.

Note that there are other ways to simplify the fractions. On the GRE, especially with fractions, you're looking for ways to cancel and simplify.

16. 36. Combine $\sqrt{9(36)+12(36)+15(36)}$ = into $\sqrt{36(36)}$, which equals 36.

17. C, D, E. If $x^2 < 25$, x is both less than 5 and greater than −5, which you can write as $-5 < x < 5$.

The value of x cannot be equal to 5 or −5. It's greater than −5 and less than 5, so from the list of answer choices, x could be equal to −3, 0, or 3.

18. B. First, find the area of the square:

$$s^2 = \left(\sqrt{2}\right)^2 = 2$$

For the area of the circle, you need its radius. Cut the square in half, corner to corner, to form two 45-45-90 triangles, where each hypotenuse is the diameter of the circle. If the side of this triangle is $\sqrt{2}$, the hypotenuse is 2, because in a right triangle, the square of the hypotenuse is the sum of the squares of the other two sides:

$$\begin{aligned} c^2 &= a^2 + b^2 \\ &= \sqrt{2}^2 + \sqrt{2}^2 \\ &= 2 + 2 \\ &= 4 \end{aligned}$$

$c^2 = 4$, so $c = \sqrt{4} = 2$ is the diameter of the circle, and the radius of the circle is half the diameter, or 1. Now for the area of the circle:

$$\pi r^2 = \pi(1)^2 = \pi$$

Subtract the area of the square from the area of the circle for your answer:

$$\pi - 2$$

19. 21. For the area of a triangle, multiply the base by the height and divide by 2. The base of this triangle is 7 and the height is 6, for an area of 21. The 2 in the drawing has no bearing.

20. A, B, C, E, F. \$600 is $\frac{1}{3}$ of \$1,800 and $\frac{1}{4}$ of \$2,400. This means that Clarissa's monthly income is greater than \$1,800 and less than \$2,400. Multiply these values by 12 for an annual income greater than \$21,600 and less than \$28,800. Note that her income can't equal these amounts: It's greater than the lower number and less than the higher number. Common trap: missing the word "not" in the question.

Block 5

Ten Tips for the Night Before the GRE

t's normal to be nervous before an important test. The tips in this block help you review helpful things you can do the night before the GRE so you're confident and ready to do your best.

Review Time-Management Strategies

Because the GRE is a timed test, a few time-management techniques can help you answer the questions you know and manage the questions you're not sure about. Don't obsess over giving each question a specific number of seconds, but do know when to give up and come back to a question later. A good rule of thumb is about a minute per question. As long as you haven't exited the section, you can return to any question in that section. Simply call up the Review Screen by clicking Review, click the question you want to return to, and then click Go to Question. You can mark a question for review so it's flagged on the Review Screen, or you can write down the question number on your scratch paper. Just keep in mind that while you're on the Review Screen, the clock still ticks.

Refresh Your Guessing Strategies

Remember that the GRE doesn't deduct points for wrong answers, so when you're running out of time and you're still not sure about the correct answer to a question, you should take your best guess. If you can eliminate any obviously wrong answers first, you improve your chances of guessing the right answer.

Plan to Wear Layers

Dress in layers. Testing centers can be warm or, more typically, cold. Shivering for hours won't help your performance. Dress in layers so you can be comfortable regardless of how they run the A/C.

Have Your Valid ID Ready

When you arrive at the testing center, you must show a valid ID before you can take the test. Make sure you know where you ID is the night before. Your identification needs three key elements:

>> A recognizable photo

>> The name you used to register for the test

>> Your signature

Usually, a driver's license, passport, employee ID, or military ID does the trick. A student ID alone isn't enough (although it works as a second form of ID in case something's unclear on your first one). Note that a Social Security card or a credit card isn't acceptable identification.

Eat Well

Certain foods and beverages affect your cognitive ability, so avoid highly processed foods and foods high in sugar, starch, or fat. These foods tend to make you feel sluggish or result in bursts of energy followed by prolonged crashes. Lean more toward veggies — especially green, leafy veggies — and foods that are high in protein. When it comes to carbohydrates, go for complex over simple. Complex carbohydrates are typically found in fresh fruits, veggies, and whole-grain products. Avoid simple carbohydrates found in candy, soda, anything made from white flour, and most junk foods, including chips. And forget those energy drinks that combine huge amounts of caffeine and sugar to get you to a state of heightened tension.

Know the Exam Software

If you placed Ernest Hemingway in front of Microsoft Word, would he be able to write anything? Probably not, even though he's one of the most noted authors of our time. For him, the problem wouldn't be the writing; it would be the software. The same applies to you: You can answer the questions, but the software is another story. How do you mark questions to return to? How do you call up the calculator? How do you check the clock? Where is the back button? Does that button end the section? The software is easy to learn, but you have enough on your mind during the exam. Master the software *before* the exam.

TIP

To check out the software, take at least one ETS GRE practice test at www.ets.org/gre/test-takers/general-test/prepare/powerprep.html. It's free and it looks and feels exactly like the real thing, providing you with a more genuine simulation.

Review Your Route to the Testing Center

You may have chosen your route already but be sure to review it. Knowing where you're going in advance will help you stay calm and confident on test day. Map your directions, and if you're driving, check your favoring mapping app for roads closed due to construction or train lines closed for maintenance. Also, if you're driving, use satellite view so you can see where to park. If you have time, you could drive to the testing center to check out the drive time, parking, fees, and so on. If you're taking public transportation, find out where and when you need to board the bus or train, how long the ride is, how much it costs, and where you get off.

TIP

If you plan to use Uber or Lyft, be sure to set the ride time to *the morning of the exam* so the trip time reflects the traffic. It doesn't hurt to plan on arriving at the testing center 30 minutes early, so if your driver or friend is late or doesn't know the roads, you have a time cushion.

Relax and Practice Your Stress Coping Skills

Relaxation comes in different forms for different people. Some folks are relaxed with friends; some read books and play music; and others practice yoga, meditation, or painting. The only requirement when choosing how to relax is making sure your brain isn't running 100 miles an hour. The whole purpose of relaxing is to give your brain a rest. So, find an activity you enjoy, thank your brain by telling it to take some time off, and recharge.

REMEMBER

Relaxation isn't a luxury — it's a requirement for success on the GRE (and a well-balanced life). You're a multifaceted human, not a work-and-study automaton.

WARNING

I've seen students who are so overextended and overachieving that they exhaust themselves before the test. They feel fine, but their performance drops like a rock. One sure sign of this is overanalyzing easy questions. Another is making simple math mistakes, such as $2 + 1 = 5$. This is real, and it happens to *everyone*.

If you feel your mind whirring the night before the test, do something to relax. If you tend to feel anxious during a test, identify what helps you center yourself. A 4-7-8 breath helps many people: Breathe in through your nose for a count of four, hold it for a count of seven, and then breathe out for a count of eight.

Review Your Areas of Focus

Do you miss more Reading Comprehension or Text Completion questions? Do you handle triangles better than you do exponents? Do you lose steam (causing your performance to drop) halfway through the exam? Do you run out of time? The practice exam can give you a sense of how you work and where you need to focus.

TIP

If you can't resist the urge to review the night before the test, review the skills needed in your weakest areas. This approach may help you navigate a tricky question on test day.

Visualize Success!

Visualizing yourself successfully taking the test on test day can put you at ease the night before the test. See yourself enter the testing room, sit down at the computer, and answer questions you've practiced on-screen. You could even imagine your favorite person or character celebrating your right answers (although the testing software doesn't have this feature, this is in your imagination!). If you repeat this visualization in your mind over and over again, you'll feel more at ease so you can rest well and be ready for the GRE the next day.

Index

About the Authors

Ron Woldoff completed his dual master's degrees at Arizona State University and San Diego State University, where he studied the culmination of business and technology. After working as a corporate consultant, Ron opened his own company, National Test Prep, to help students reach their goals on college entrance exams. He created the programs and curricula for these tests from scratch, using his own observations of the tests and feedback from students.

Ron has instructed his own GMAT and GRE programs at both Northern Arizona University and the internationally acclaimed Thunderbird School of Global Management. Ron has also assisted at various high schools, where he led student groups and coached student instructors to help others prepare for the SAT, ACT, and PSAT. Ron lives in Phoenix, Arizona, with his lovely wife, Leisah, and their three amazing boys, Zachary, Jadon, and Adam. You can find Ron on the web at http://testprepaz.com.

Publisher's Acknowledgments

Executive Editor: Lindsay Lefevere

Compiling Editor: Rebecca Huehls

Editor: Elizabeth Kuball

Proofreader: Debbye Butler

Production Editor: Tamilmani Varadharaj

Cover Design: Wiley

Cover Image: © bortonia/Getty Images

Leverage the power

Dummies is the global leader in the reference category and one of the most trusted and highly regarded brands in the world. No longer just focused on books, customers now have access to the dummies content they need in the format they want. Together we'll craft a solution that engages your customers, stands out from the competition, and helps you meet your goals.

Advertising & Sponsorships

Connect with an engaged audience on a powerful multimedia site, and position your message alongside expert how-to content. Dummies.com is a one-stop shop for free, online information and know-how curated by a team of experts.

- Targeted ads
- Video
- Email Marketing
- Microsites
- Sweepstakes sponsorship

20 MILLION PAGE VIEWS EVERY SINGLE MONTH

15 MILLION UNIQUE VISITORS PER MONTH

43% OF ALL VISITORS ACCESS THE SITE VIA THEIR MOBILE DEVICES

700,000 NEWSLETTER SUBSCRIPTIONS TO THE INBOXES OF **300,000** UNIQUE INDIVIDUALS EVERY WEEK

# of dummies

Custom Publishing

Reach a global audience in any language by creating a solution that will differentiate you from competitors, amplify your message, and encourage customers to make a buying decision.

- Apps
- Books
- eBooks
- Video
- Audio
- Webinars

Brand Licensing & Content

Leverage the strength of the world's most popular reference brand to reach new audiences and channels of distribution.

For more information, visit **dummies.com/biz**

PERSONAL ENRICHMENT

Staying Sharp	**Facebook**	**Guitar**	**Investing**	**Beekeeping**	**Digital Photography**
9781119187790	9781119179030	9781119293354	9781119293347	9781119310068	9781119235606
USA $26.00	USA $21.99	USA $24.99	USA $22.99	USA $22.99	USA $24.99
CAN $31.99	CAN $25.99	CAN $29.99	CAN $27.99	CAN $27.99	CAN $29.99
UK £19.99	UK £16.99	UK £17.99	UK £16.99	UK £16.99	UK £17.99
Meditation	**Pregnancy**	**Samsung Galaxy S7**	**iPhone**	**Crocheting**	**Nutrition**
9781119251163	9781119235491	9781119279952	9781119283133	9781119287117	9781119130246
USA $24.99	USA $26.99	USA $24.99	USA $24.99	USA $24.99	USA $22.99
CAN $29.99	CAN $31.99	CAN $29.99	CAN $29.99	CAN $29.99	CAN $27.99
UK £17.99	UK £19.99	UK £17.99	UK £17.99	UK £16.99	UK £16.99

PROFESSIONAL DEVELOPMENT

Windows 10	**AutoCAD**	**Excel 2016**	**QuickBooks 2017**	**macOS Sierra**	**LinkedIn**	**Windows 10**
9781119311041	9781119255796	9781119293439	9781119281467	9781119280651	9781119251132	9781119310563
USA $24.99	USA $39.99	USA $26.99	USA $26.99	USA $29.99	USA $24.99	USA $34.00
CAN $29.99	CAN $47.99	CAN $31.99	CAN $31.99	CAN $35.99	CAN $29.99	CAN $41.99
UK £17.99	UK £27.99	UK £19.99	UK £19.99	UK £21.99	UK £17.99	UK £24.99
SharePoint 2016	**Fundamental Analysis**	**Networking**	**Office 2016**	**Office 365**	**Salesforce.com**	**Coding**
9781119181705	9781119263593	9781119257769	9781119293477	9781119265313	9781119239314	9781119293323
USA $29.99	USA $26.99	USA $29.99	USA $26.99	USA $24.99	USA $29.99	USA $29.99
CAN $35.99	CAN $31.99	CAN $35.99	CAN $31.99	CAN $29.99	CAN $35.99	CAN $35.99
UK £21.99	UK £19.99	UK £21.99	UK £19.99	UK £17.99	UK £21.99	UK £21.99

Learning Made Easy

ACADEMIC

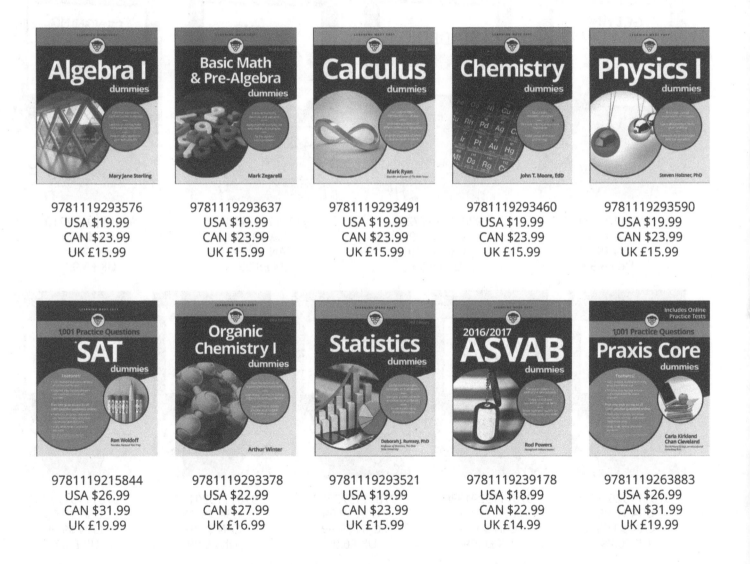

Algebra I dummies
Mary Jane Sterling
9781119293576
USA $19.99
CAN $23.99
UK £15.99

Basic Math & Pre-Algebra dummies
Mark Zegarelli
9781119293637
USA $19.99
CAN $23.99
UK £15.99

Calculus dummies
Mark Ryan
9781119293491
USA $19.99
CAN $23.99
UK £15.99

Chemistry dummies
John T. Moore, EdD
9781119293460
USA $19.99
CAN $23.99
UK £15.99

Physics I dummies
Steven Holzner, PhD
9781119293590
USA $19.99
CAN $23.99
UK £15.99

1,001 Practice Questions
SAT dummies
Ron Woldoff
9781119215844
USA $26.99
CAN $31.99
UK £19.99

Organic Chemistry I dummies
Arthur Winter
9781119293378
USA $22.99
CAN $27.99
UK £16.99

Statistics dummies
Deborah J. Rumsey, PhD
9781119293521
USA $19.99
CAN $23.99
UK £15.99

2016/2017
ASVAB dummies
Rod Powers
9781119239178
USA $18.99
CAN $22.99
UK £14.99

Includes Online Practice Tests
1,001 Practice Questions
Praxis Core dummies
Carla Kirkland
Chan Cleveland
9781119263883
USA $26.99
CAN $31.99
UK £19.99

Available Everywhere Books Are Sold

dummies.com